JOB

A SELF-STUDY GUIDE

Irving L. Jensen

MOODY PRESS

CHICAGO

Cover photo: Drawing water from a well in the region of Gibeah

ISBN: 0-8024-4479-2

1 2 3 4 5 6 Printing/EP/Year 95 94 93 92 91

Contents

Introduction

Does justice triumph?
What is God really like?
Is God actively concerned about the lives of His children?
Why are some godly people crushed with tragedy?
What are the enduring values in life?
Is there life beyond the grave?
Is Satan real?

These are solemn questions that have been asked by people who believe in God and are facing the complex *problem of pain.*

The fact that God inspired a book like Job to be written and included in the canon of the Holy Bible is strong evidence of His love for His children. Here are His perfect answers to the many agonizing questions about life. Every Christian who reads and studies the book of Job will learn to know God better and will discover truths about the kind of faith that God wants His children to exercise concerning severe trials and testings. Peter's words bringing Christ into the picture will shine forth in all their splendor:

> That the trial of your faith, being much more precious than of gold that perisheth, though it be tried with fire, might be found unto praise and honour and glory at the appearing of Jesus Christ. (1 Pet. 1:7)

Suggestions for Study

Here are a few suggestions that will help make your study of Job most profitable.

1. Use a Bible that has good paper and wide margins, so that you can make notations on its pages.

2. If possible use an edition of the Bible that prints the text of Job in a single column, line by line, in the form of poetry.[1] (This format is used in the *New American Standard Bible.*)

3. Approach the book of Job with a desire to learn.

4. Be willing to invest time—that precious commodity—in this study.

5. Study methodically, following the directions in this manual. Method is simply orderly procedure.

6. Concentration is a must.

7. Be word-and-phrase-conscious in all of your analyses.

8. Always look for key teachings in the biblical text.

9. Observe not only *what* the Bible says (content) but *how* it says it (structure).

10. Keep a pencil in hand while you study. Record your observations.

11. Don't lose sight of your spiritual goals in studying God's Word. (Recall one of David's goals: Psalm 119:11.)

1. The version quoted in this manual is the King James (KJV), unless otherwise specified. Permission to quote extensively from the *New American Standard Bible* © 1960, 1962, 1963, 1968, 1971, has been granted by the Lockman Foundation.

Lesson 1
Background of Job

Why suffering and catastrophe fall upon good people has puzzled mankind throughout the centuries. In our study of Job we will learn what God wants His children to know about this vexing problem, and how they can find perfect peace.

Before we study the text itself, let us look into the background of the book. This is the best procedure to follow in studying any book of the Bible. We will proceed according to this basic order of study: (1) background and setting; (2) survey of the entire book; and (3) analysis of the individual parts.

Lesson 2 is devoted to survey, and the remaining lessons concentrate on analysis, which is the core of Bible book study.

The book of Job was written long ago. In order to gain a thorough understanding of it, the modern reader must look into such matters as its setting, its author, the persons mentioned in it, and why it was written. It is true that you can profitably study the Bible without delving into this background information. Knowing it will, however, deepen your comprehension of the truths revealed in the Bible.

I. THE MAN JOB

A. Name

There are two possible meanings for the name *Job*. If the name's origin is in the Arabic language, it means "one who turns back (repents)". If its origin is Hebrew, it means "the hated (persecuted) one." It is interesting that both of these meanings are reflected in experiences of Job as recorded in the book bearing his name.

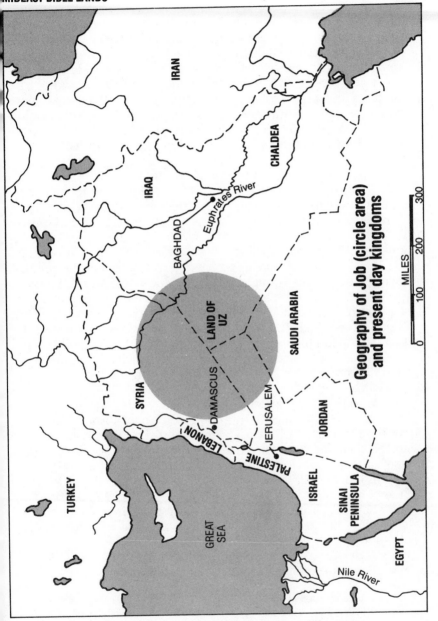

Geography of Job (circle area) and present day kingdoms

7

B. Biography and Descriptions

Job was a real person, not a fictitious character, as some critics contend. Read Ezekiel 14:14-20 and James 5:11 for clear evidence of this. Since we have little biographical information about Job, we can make only a few general statements about his background.

1. Job was a native of the land of Uz (1:1). This region was located northeast of Palestine, near desert land (1:19), probably between the city of Damascus and the Euphrates River. This would place the region near the borders of modern Iraq and Saudi Arabia. (See map, Chart A.) Read 1:3 and note that Job was from an area called "the east."

2. Job probably lived before or around the time of Abraham. This is suggested by the fact that the book of Job does not mention Israel's covenant relationship with God, which is the core of Hebrew history from the call of Abraham (Gen. 12) onward.[1] Also there is no reference to Hebrew institutions (e.g., the law). The kind of sacrifice described in 1:5 was practiced before or outside the Mosaic order of worship, according to which only the priests sacrificed offerings brought by the people (Ex. 20:44).[2] We may say, therefore, that the man Job lived between the construction of the Tower of Babel and the call of Abraham, or shortly thereafter.[3] Read Genesis 11:9–12:1 to fix in your mind this chronological setting. Then read the words of God in Job 39 and note the different kinds of animals, including the horse, with which Job was familiar. Man's habitat has not changed radically during the long course of world history.

3. Some have suggested that Job had reached the age of sixty when the events related in this book took place. Whatever his age, we know nothing of his earlier life. Questions that remain unanswered include: Who were his parents? From whom did he first learn about God? How widespread was his witness for God?

4. Job was very wealthy. Read 1:3, 10. He and his sons were homeowners in a large city of the region (cf. 1:4; 29:7). Archaeologists have discovered the ruins of more than three hundred ancient cities in the area of Uz, which indicates that a flourishing civilization existed in those early days.

5. He was a respected and popular judge and benefactor of his fellow citizens (29:7-25).

---

1. If Job was a contemporary of Abraham, or lived after him, then he was a believer outside the covenant family of Israel. (Cf. Acts 14:17.)
2. The "burnt offerings" of 1:5 are not Levitical offerings, according to this view.
3. References to a Job appear in extrabiblical texts dated as early as 2000 B.C. The footnote in the *Berkeley Version* at 42:16-17 reads, "His many years suggest the period of Abraham."

6. He was righteous in God's eyes. Read 1:1, 5, 8. Compare also Ezekiel 14:14-20 and James 5:11. What does the last phrase of Job 1:5 suggest about his relationship to God?

7. He lived to a ripe old age. If Job was as old as 60 when he was first tested (chap. 1), then he was at least 200 years old when he died (42:16-17). Compare this with the ages of the people listed in Genesis 11:10-26 (cf. also Gen. 25:7).

As you study the book of Job, you will become better acquainted with Job as a person.

II. THE BOOK OF JOB

A. Title

The book is named for its main character, not for its author. The book of Ruth is an example of another writing so named.

B. Author and Date

The human author is anonymous and the date of writing uncertain.[4] Such is the case for many books of the Bible. Among those suggested as writer are Moses, Solomon, a contemporary of Solomon (cf. 1 Kings 4:29-34), Isaiah, Jeremiah, Baruch, a prophet of the captivity, and Job. Most scholars agree that the author lived at a time later than Abraham. If he was a contemporary of Solomon, an approximate date of writing would be 950 B.C. One writer supports an early date before the prophets:

> The grandeur and spontaneity of the book and its deeply empathic re-creation of the sentiments of men standing early in the progress of revelation point to the early pre-Exilic period, before the doctrinal, especially the eschatological, contribution of the prophets.[5]

Chart B shows the historical context of possible dates for the man Job and the book written about him.

The book's authority and dependability rest not on human authorship but on divine authorship. Only God could reveal the conversation between Himself and Satan, recorded in chapters 1-2.

4. The uncertainty regarding human authorship and date does not limit our study of this remarkable Old Testament book.
5. Meredith G. Kline, "Job," in *The Wycliffe Bible Commentary*, p. 460.

POSSIBLE DATES OF JOB IN HISTORICAL CONTEXT

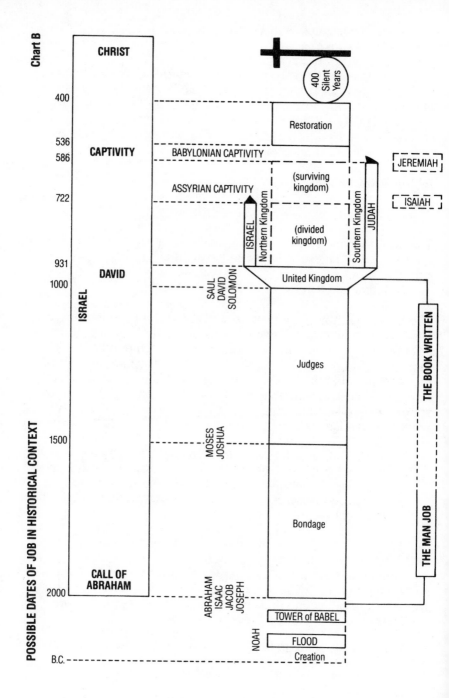

C. Purposes

Job is a book about a physical and spiritual experience of an ancient patriarch whose faith was tested to the uttermost. Its main purposes are not to teach Israelite history, messianic prophecy, the ABC's of salvation, or the mission of the church. These are the big tasks of other parts of Scripture. The underlying purposes of Job are the following:

1. To reveal who God is.

2. To show the kind of trust He wants His children to have. (For example: Trust God even though you cannot fully account for your circumstances.) Approval by God means "tried and true" (cf. Rom. 16:10, *Berkeley*).

3. To reveal His favor toward His children and His absolute control over Satan.

4. To answer man's questions about why a righteous person may suffer while an evil man may enjoy health and prosperity.

The entire book of Job is concerned with the problem of pain. The answer to the problem that is stated in number 4 above is contained in the first three statements: who God is determines what He does; therefore we must trust Him without reservation.

D. Doctrinal Content

The book of Job makes reference, directly or indirectly, to most of the key doctrines of the Bible, including God; man; Satan; sin and righteousness; affliction, discipline, and blessing; justice; faith; and nature. Many references to God's creation appear throughout the book. Included are astronomical facts, such as names of stars and constellations (38:31-32), suspension of the earth in space (26:7), and the spherical shape of the earth (22:14). (Scan chaps. 38 and 39, which are filled with similar references.)

The contents of the book are surveyed in Lesson 2. Does it surprise you that such a great variety of truth was revealed to men of God even before the Scriptures were recorded?

E. Style

Job is classified as dramatic poetry. The book is recognized even in the world of secular literature as a magnificent dramatic poem. Thomas Carlyle, a Scottish essayist and historian (1795-1881), wrote, "There is nothing written, I think, in the Bible or out of it, of equal literary merit."

Poetry is the language of the heart. Thus Job describes the innermost thoughts of men, more so than their actions. The poetic section of the book (3:1–42:6) uses a poetic device called parallelism. The three most common kinds of parallelism are:

1. Synonymous: a thought is stated in the first line, then repeated in similar language in the second. (Most parallelism in Job is of this kind.)
   Example: "By the blast of God they perish, and by the breath of his nostrils are they consumed" (4:9).
2. Antithetic: the statement in the first line is followed by a contrasting statement of the second line.
   Example: "My friends scorn me:
       But mine eye poureth out tears unto God" (16:20).
3. Synthetic: a number of related thoughts expand on the statement of the first line.
   Example: Read 4:19-21.

In drama, not everything spoken by the actors is necessarily true. Likewise in the book of Job. For example, Job's three friends, Eliphaz, Bildad, and Zophar, give their own interpretations of Job's afflictions. Later they are rebuked by God for not speaking "the thing that is right" (42:7). (The speeches of Job's three friends take up eight chapters of the book.)

F. Relation to Other Books of the Bible

Job is the first of the five poetic books of the Bible. The books before it, from Genesis to Esther, are for the most part historical in nature. If Job lived before or outside the Abrahamic setting, as suggested earlier in this lesson, an interesting comparison may be made between the poetical and historical books. This is shown on Chart C.

The book of Job is intimately related to the New Testament, even though it is explicitly quoted only once (1 Cor. 3:19 quoting Job 5:13). The problems and questions of the man Job are answered completely and perfectly in Christ. G. Campbell Morgan cites nine such answers and confirmations of Jesus.[6] Read the verses listed below and ponder the blessed truth that Jesus is the complete and only answer to every need of modern man.

6. G. Campbell Morgan, *The Answers of Jesus to Job*, p. 5.

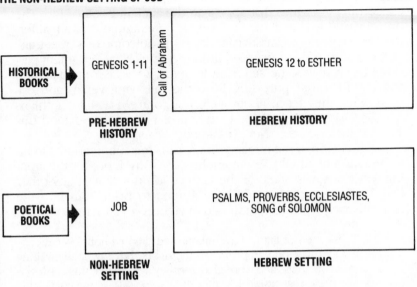

Subject	Book of Job	Answered and Confirmed in Jesus
1. Cry for a daysman (mediator)	9:33	1 Timothy 2:5
2. Inquiry about life	14:14	John 11:25
3. Witness in heaven	16:19	Hebrews 9:24
4. Living redeemer	19:25	Hebrews 7:25
5. Quest for God	23:3	John 14:9
6. Challenge to God	31:35	Hebrews 12:22-24
7. Discovery of self	40:4	Matthew 16:26; John 3:16
8. Discovery of God	42:5-6	Matthew 4:17
9. Sense of solution	23:10	James 1:12

The New Testament gives the complete and final revelation concerning doctrines that appear in the ancient book of Job. The prominent doctrine about suffering is an example. Not all suffering experienced by Christians today is the outcome of a "meeting" of Satan and God, as recorded in Job. Various New Testament passages teach that some suffering is penal, some is remedial, and some is for other purposes. Read the following verses and observe what they teach about suffering: John 9:1-2; 1 Corinthians 11:29-32; Hebrews 12:7-11; 1 Peter 4:12-14. You can extend this study to include other New Testament verses.

It is clear that the ministry of Christ is the culmination and interpretation of all Old Testament history. Were it not for the atoning work of Christ, neither the faith of Job nor that of any other Old Testament saint would have availed to bring him into the heavenly city, which is mentioned in Hebrews 11:13-16:

> These men of faith I have mentioned died without ever receiving all that God had promised them; but they saw it all awaiting them on ahead and were glad, for they agreed that this earth was not their real home but that they were just strangers visiting down here. And quite obviously when they talked like that they were looking forward to their real home in heaven. . . . And now God is not ashamed to be called their God, for **he has made a heavenly city for them** (TLB,⁷ bold added).

* * *

REVIEW QUESTIONS:

1. What is the value of studying the background of a biblical book before analyzing its text? Did the original readers of each book know the background of the writing addressed to them?

2. What are the two possible meanings of the name "Job"?

3. What are the evidences that Job was a real person?

4. What do you know about Job's native land?

5. Give reasons to support the theory that Job lived shortly before or around the time of Abraham.

6. How did God describe Job's spiritual condition before his affliction?

7. Account for the title of the book of Job, assuming that Job did not write it.

8. State some of the views concerning the authorship of the book.

7. *The Living Bible.*

9. In your own words, what are the main purposes of the book of Job?

10. What are some of the outstanding subjects discussed in the book?

11. Compare the contents of Job with that of other poetical books.

12. Cite biblical passages that show Jesus is the perfect answer to the needs of men like Job.

13. What, in your opinion, are some of the Christian graces that may be strengthened through suffering and adversity?

Lesson 2
Survey of Job

To fully appreciate any of the marvels of God's handiwork, we must examine it thoroughly. Examining a rose, we first admire the entire blossom, and then we recognize the beauty of its individual parts. This is as it should be. Pliny the Elder, the great naturalist of the first century, made this observation: "The power and greatness of the works of nature lose of their true comprehension in nearly every instance when the mind seizes on particulars and does not embrace the whole."

In studying Job, we will follow the procedure of moving from the whole to the parts, from the general to the particular. In this lesson we will take a panoramic view of the book of Job to see its highlights and major movements. In the following lessons we will analyze the individual chapters in detail. If we were to read one of the speeches of Job's three friends without relating it to the total story, which includes the origin of Job's plight (chaps. 1-2) and God's commentary on the three friends' interpretations (e.g., 42:7), we might reach incorrect conclusions.

I. A FIRST SCANNING

1. How many chapters are in the book?
2. Scan the opening phrases of the chapters. Would you say the book mainly relates action or discourse? Where in the book do the speeches begin, and where do they end? The format used in the *New American Standard Bible* (NASB) is excellent for a study of Job. The prose (narrative) is printed in the usual style, and the speeches, which are dramatic poetry, are printed in stanzas composed of single lines.

THE SPEAKERS IN THE DRAMA OF JOB

Chap.	JOB	ELIPHAZ	BILDAD	ZOPHAR	Chap.	JOB	ELIHU	GOD
3	X				32			
4		X			33			
5		X			34			
6					35			
7					36			
8					37			
9					38			
10					39			
11					40:1			
12					40:3			
13					40:6			
14					41:1			
15					42:1			
16								
17								
18								
19								
20								
21								
22								
23								
24								
25								
26								
27								
28								
29								
30								
31								

17

II. CHAPTER CONTENT

Now scan the book again and identify more specifically the content of each chapter. For the speeches (3:1–42:6) you need only note who the speakers are. Sometimes a speech covers more than one chapter (e.g., Eliphaz's speech of chaps. 4-5). In only two chapters of the poetic section are speeches shorter than a full chapter (see chaps. 40, 42). Record your survey of the speeches on the work sheet (Chart D).

You may wonder why such a large portion of the book is devoted to the mistaken diagnoses and arguments of Job's three friends. If their main charge was that Job's personal sins caused his suffering, do you suppose that they were afraid of the same kind of suffering befalling them? If so, may this partly explain their persistence in dealing with Job?

III. SURVEY CHART

Chart E is a survey of Job, showing by various outlines how the book is organized. You may want to add outlines of your own, as you proceed with this study.

Refer to this chart as you make the following observations and complete the study suggestions:

1. Note how the book opens (Job Before the Trial) and how it closes (Job After the Trial). Read the biblical references.

2. Observe the three-part outline of style at the top of the chart.

3. Study the outlines shown below the base line. Compare these outlines with your own survey outlines. You may need to scan the biblical text at some places to verify an outline. Justify the location of main divisions at 38:1; 40:3; and 42:7.

4. What is the basis for dividing the controversies of chapters 4-31 into three cycles? (Refer to your work sheet, Chart D.)

5. Observe the progression at the bottom of the chart, beginning with The Problem of Pain.

6. Note the key verse, title, and key words assigned to this book. Formulate similar items as you proceed in the lessons that follow.

7. Read the following choice passages of Job at this time: 1:21; 5:17; 14:14; 16:21; 19:23-27; 26:7-14; 28:12-28; 42:1-6.

IV. JOB'S THREE FRIENDS AND ELIHU

Thus far we have not said much about Elihu and "Job's three friends"—Eliphaz, Bildad, and Zophar. Read 2:11-13 and 32:1-5 for

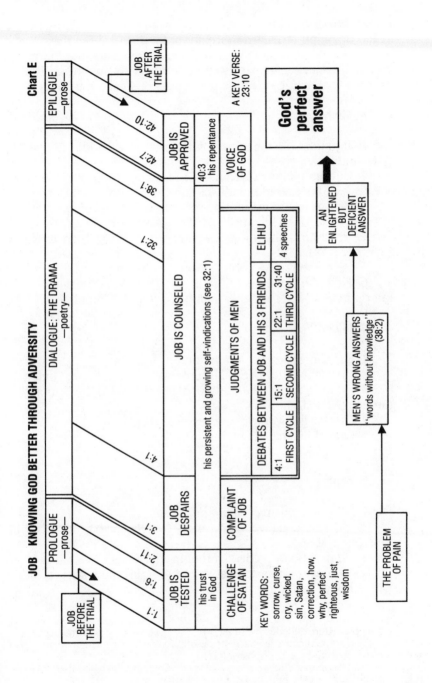

JOB KNOWING GOD BETTER THROUGH ADVERSITY

Chart E

| JOB BEFORE THE TRIAL | PROLOGUE —prose— | DIALOGUE: THE DRAMA —poetry— | | | EPILOGUE —prose— | JOB AFTER THE TRIAL |

PROLOGUE —prose—
1:1 / 1:6 / 2:11 / 3:1

JOB IS TESTED
his trust in God
CHALLENGE OF SATAN

JOB DESPAIRS
COMPLAINT OF JOB

DIALOGUE: THE DRAMA —poetry—
4:1 / 32:1 / 38:1 / 42:7 / 42:10

JOB IS COUNSELED
his persistent and growing self-vindications (see 32:1)

JUDGMENTS OF MEN

DEBATES BETWEEN JOB AND HIS 3 FRIENDS
4:1 FIRST CYCLE | 15:1 SECOND CYCLE | 22:1 31:40 THIRD CYCLE

ELIHU
4 speeches

VOICE OF GOD
40:3 his repentance

JOB IS APPROVED

A KEY VERSE: 23:10

KEY WORDS:
sorrow, curse, cry, wicked, sin, Satan, correction, how, why, perfect, righteous, just, wisdom

THE PROBLEM OF PAIN → MEN'S WRONG ANSWERS "words without knowledge" (38:2) → AN ENLIGHTENED BUT DEFICIENT ANSWER → **God's perfect answer**

19

a brief introduction to these men. Since they are key characters, it would be helpful to learn more about them and about their views on life before we begin the analytical studies. Study the following descriptions and refer back to this summary during the course of your study.[1] Enlarge or revise the descriptions along the way.

A. Eliphaz

1. Two possible meanings of the name are "God is fine gold" and "God is dispenser."
2. He was a native of Teman (2:11), a city in Edom, southeast of Palestine. It was traditionally famous for its wise men (Jer. 49:7).
3. He acts as the leading spokesman for the three friends.
4. He is the "scientist" of the group; his speeches show clearer reasoning and more considerate criticism than those of the other two friends.
5. He is seen to be noble, sincere, wise, and courtly.
6. Two of his main contentions are that God is perfectly pure and righteous (4:17) and that man brings trouble on himself (5:7).

B. Bildad

1. His name means "son of contention."
2. He was a native of Shuah (Sukhu of the Euphrates region?).
3. He may be called a traditionalist (cf. 8:8-10); he is more argumentative than Eliphaz.
4. He charges Job with godlessness (8:13).
5. One of his main contentions is that God never twists justice (8:3).

C. Zophar

1. His name means "hairy" or "rough."
2. He was a native of Naamah (or Naamath), probably in northern Arabia.
3. He may be the oldest of the three friends.[2]
4. A blunt-spoken dogmatist and moralist, he sometimes displays a holier-than-thou attitude.

---

1. This procedure is deductive in nature. If we followed the inductive approach here, we would arrive at character descriptions of the four men *after* we had completed studying the book of Job.
2. Some believe that Eliphaz was the oldest of the three men, and therefore oriental courtesy gave him the right to speak first.

5. He charges Job with boasting (11:2-6, NASB).

6. One of his main contentions is that God knows iniquity when He sees it (11:11).

D. Elihu

1. His name means "He is my God."

2. He was a native of Buz (possibly in Arabia or Syria).

3. The youngest of the four men, he is not an intimate companion of Job's three friends.

4. One of his main contentions is that God is good (33:24). Of the four men, Elihu gives the best diagnosis of Job's plight, saying that sufferings are often God's way of refining the righteous. He does not go far enough in his diagnosis, however.

V. SUMMARY OF THE THEME OF JOB

The theme of the book of Job is summarized below, in four parts. (Recall the outline at the bottom of Chart E.)

1. The problem of pain: Why do the righteous suffer and the wicked prosper?

2. The wrong answer of Job's three friends: Suffering is God's judgment for sin.

3. The enlightened answer of Elihu: Suffering is God's way to teach, discipline, and refine.

4. God's perfect answer: Suffering is a test of trusting God for who He is and not for what He does.

In the following lessons we will look for the development of this theme in the drama of Job.

Lesson 3

Job's First Trials

The two opening chapters in Job teach some of the most basic doctrines about man and God. The question that the remainder of the book discusses, "Why does righteous Job suffer?" is factually answered in chapters 1-2. Job's first tests are the subject of our present lesson.

The persons and events mentioned in the first two chapters of Job are real persons and actual events. "There was a man. . . . Now there was a day. . . . So . . . Satan . . . smote Job" (1:1, 6; 2:7). This is precise, genuine history. And, lest we think that Satan is no longer active in accusing the children of God, the last book of the Bible reveals the sober truth that Satan's work will continue until end times: "The accuser of our brethren is cast down, which accused them before our God day and night" (Rev. 12:10). The consolation for the Christian in his daily walk is found in Christ's intercessory ministry revealed by His warm words to Simon Peter: "Simon, Simon, behold, Satan has demanded *permission* to sift you like wheat; but I have prayed for you, that your faith may not fail" (Luke 22:31-32, NASB).

I. PREPARATION FOR STUDY

1. Review the geographical locations noted in lesson 1. Refer to the map (Chart A) to establish in your mind the setting of this chapter. Note the location of Chaldea (cf. 1:17). The "Sabeans" mentioned in 1:15 were Arab bedouin.[1]

2. Satan first appears in the story of man in the Garden of Eden. Read the account of his beguiling Eve (Gen. 3:1-7). The text

---

1. A footnote on this verse in *Today's English Version* (TEV) identifies the Sabeans as a tribe of wandering raiders from the south, and the Chaldeans as a tribe of wandering raiders from the north.

refers to him as "the serpent." How do you know that this was Satan? (Cf. Rev. 12:9.) Why is Satan anti-humankind? The name "Satan" means literally "adversary." Of its nineteen appearances in the Old Testament, fourteen are in Job. The name "devil" means "slanderer" and is found only in the New Testament (60 times).

II. ANALYSIS

Segment to be analyzed: 1:1-22
Paragraph divisions: at verses 1:1, 6, 13, 20

A. General Analysis

1. First mark the paragraph divisions in your Bible. Then read the chapter for general impressions. Get in the habit of marking key words and phrases in your Bible as you read. This will enlarge the field of your vision. As someone once said, "The pencil is one of the best eyes."

2. Record key words and phrases in the boxes of Chart F. Use this chart as a work sheet for recording other observations as well.

3. What title would you give this chapter? Record it at the top of the chart. Is there a key phrase or verse in the chapter that represents this title?

4. Why are the first and fourth paragraphs on the chart set off from the second and third?

5. Complete the comparative outline about Job (right-hand margin). Complete also the outline "Trial."

6. Who are the main characters in each part of the chapter? Indicate this in the narrow left-hand column.

7. Compare the spiritual state of Job in the opening verses with that in the concluding verse.

B. Paragraph Analysis

1. *Paragraph 1:1-5*
List everything that you learn from this paragraph about Job's character and spiritual life. What does the word "perfect" mean? Compare Genesis 6:9.

_____

_____

_____

TITLE:

	JOB AND HIS FAMILY			JOB, RICH AND BLESSED
	1			
THE TRIAL PROPOSED (scene in heaven)	6			
THE TRIAL . . . . . . (scene on earth)	13			
	20			JOB, BANKRUPT AND . . . . . .
	22			

24

What additional description of Job is given in Job 1:8, in the words of the Lord?

_____

What do you learn about Job from the phrase "thus did Job continually" (1:5)?

_____

_____

What question did Job have in his mind concerning the feasts that his sons were accustomed to holding?

_____

How would you describe Job's ministry (referred to as "sanctified . . . offered burnt offerings")?

_____

Do you think his ministry was acceptable to God?

_____

_____

2. *Paragraph 1:6-12*
Who first suggested that God test Job's spiritual integrity?

_____

What was Satan's response to God's favorable evaluation of Job's heart?

_____

_____

What permission did God grant to Satan?

_____

To what extent was it limited?

_____

Who would control the testing experience?

3. *Paragraph 1:13-20*
What were the four reports brought to Job by his servants?

_____

_____

_____

_____

How much time elapsed between the arrival of the four messages (cf. 1:16, 17, 18)?

Which report was the most grievous?

What event was transpiring while these trials were inflicted?

Does this explain why the information of 1:4-5 was included in the opening paragraph?

4. *Paragraph 1:20-22*
List the six verbs in 1:20-21a. What does each word reveal about Job's reaction upon hearing the tragic news of disaster?

Analyze the spoken words of Job (1:21). What does he recognize in the first part of the verse (subject being "I")?

Compare 1 Timothy 6:7. How is this extended in the second part (subject being "the Lord")?

Describe Job's heart attitude as revealed in the last statement of the verse.

Compare this ascription of praise with Satan's prediction in 1:11b.

Note the following renderings of the last phrase of verse 22:
    (a) "Nor charged God of doing wrong" (*Berkeley*[2]).
    (b) "Did not . . . revile God" (TLB).
    (c) "Nor did he blame God" (NASB).

2. *Berkeley Version in Modern English.*

Did Job know about the conversation between Satan and God (1:6-12)? In what sense would such knowledge have nullified the test?

_____

_____

How does this paragraph illustrate the observation that bruised hearts often emit the sweetest fragrance?

_____

III. NOTES

1. *"Perfect"* (1:1). When used in the Bible to describe a man's spiritual state, this word does not mean sinless but complete, without hypocrisy, possessing integrity (cf. James 1:4).

2. *"Greatest"* (1:3). The context supports the meaning "richest," as paraphrased in *The Living Bible* and *Today's English Version.*

3. *"Burnt offerings"* (1:5). The first animal offering mentioned in the Bible was made by Abel (Gen. 4:4). Job made burnt offerings on behalf of his sons and daughters to restore any broken fellowship between them and God. Job therefore was the family's interceding priest. The symbolism of burning was twofold: spiritual cleansing (by fire) and lifting of the heart to God in worship (ascending smoke).

4. *"Cursed God"* (1:5). The *Berkeley Version* translates this as "renounced God."

5. *"Sons of God"* (1:6). These were angels of the heavenly host (cf. 38:7).

6. *"Going to and fro in the earth"* (1:7). Satan is not omnipresent, but he can work simultaneously in the hearts of people all over the world through his subordinates—evil angels and evil spirits (Matt. 25:41; Eph. 2:2; 6:12).

IV. FOR THOUGHT AND DISCUSSION

1. What have you learned from this chapter about Satan?

2. What do you think are God's purposes in permitting Satan to exercise certain powers, limited though these powers may be?

3. Who do you suppose chose the day of trial (1:13) for Job —Satan or God? Give reasons for your answer.

4. How would you describe Job's relationship to God? What is suggested by God's words "my servant Job" (1:8)?

5. What does this chapter teach about material possessions?

6. What kind of trust in God did Job have? Ponder this statement: "A man must continue to fear God even when his world flies apart and life strands him . . . in stunned bewilderment on the refuse heap."[3]

7. Why did righteous Job suffer the loss of all his possessions and his family? Answer this in light of chapter 1.

V. FURTHER STUDY

Since Satan plays a prominent role in Job, you may want to read other Scriptures about him to get a full picture of his character and works. The following list will help you in such a study.[4]

He was disguised in the Edenic serpent, Genesis 3:1-14.

He is the serpent's seed, Genesis 3:15.

He was Lucifer, son of the morning, before his fall, Isaiah 14:12.

He was the anointed cherub that covers, Ezekiel 28:14.

He energized David to evil, 1 Chronicles 21:1.

He accused and afflicted Job, Job 1:7–2:10.

He opposes unbelieving Israel prefigured by Joshua the priest, Zechariah 3:1-9.

He is the tempter, Matthew 4:3.

He is the prince of the demons, Matthew 12:24.

He instigates false doctrine, 1 Timothy 4:1-6.

He perverts the Word of God, Matthew 4:4; Luke 4:10-11 (context).

He works in demon possession, Matthew 12:22-29.

He is Satan, the adversary, Zechariah 3:1.

He is the devil, the slanderer, Luke 4:13.

He caused Judas to betray Christ, John 13:2, 27, and Ananias to lie, Acts 5:3.

He blinds people spiritually, 2 Corinthians 4:4.

He seeks to harm believers, 1 Peter 5:8.

He heads a celestial hierarchy of evil, Ephesians 6:11-12.

He is at work in the unsaved, Ephesians 2:2, who are his "sons," John 8:44.

He works diabolic miracles, 2 Thessalonians 2:9.

He was branded "a liar" and "the father of it" by Jesus, John 8:44.

He is a murderer, John 8:44.

He is the prince of this world, John 12:31; 14; 30.

He binds people physically and spiritually, Luke 13:16.

---

3. Meredith G. Kline, "Job," in *The Wycliffe Bible Commentary*, p. 462.
4. Merrill F. Unger, *Unger's Bible Handbook*, pp. 520-21.

He is a fallen angel, Matthew 25:41.

He sows tares, Matthew 13:38-39, and snatches away the Word, Matthew 13:19.

He will be bound during the Millennium, Revelation 20:1-3.

He is "the enemy," Matthew 13:39, "the evil one," Matthew 13:38.

He is routed by Spirit-directed prayer, Ephesians 6:10-20.

He is overcome by faith, 1 Peter 5:8-9.

He hinders God's will in believers, 1 Thessalonians 2:18.

He is the deceiver, Revelation 12:9.

He is the dragon, that old serpent, Revelation 12:9; 20:2.

He fell from a sinless high estate, Luke 10:18.

He viewed Simon Peter as a target, Luke 22:31.

He has an assembly of legalists who deny God's grace in Christ, Revelation 2:9.

His children are unsaved people, 1 John 3:8, 10.

His ultimate fate is Gehenna, Matthew 25:41; Revelation 20:10.

VI. WORDS TO PONDER

> The Lord gave me everything I had,
> and they were his to take away.
> Blessed be the name of the Lord.
> (1:21, TLB)

Lesson 4
Job's Further Trial

Job maintained his integrity even when Satan moved God to destroy him without cause. This was God's report to Satan concerning the outcome of Job's first test (2:3). But Satan argued that Job had not cursed God because only his possessions had been taken. "Touch *him*—his own bone and flesh—and watch him curse you!" was Satan's new challenge. This is the story in Lesson 4, and it is a moving story indeed.

I. PREPARATION FOR STUDY

1. Since this narrative forms the natural sequel to chapter 1, review that chapter briefly. Especially note such phrases as "there was a day" and "hast thou considered my servant Job?" They will reappear in chapter 2.

COMPARISONS OF JOB'S TWO TRIALS   Chart G

Chapter 1	Chapter 2
FIRST TRIALS	**FURTHER TRIALS**
BANKRUPTCY & BEREAVEMENT	PHYSICAL PAIN
TOUCH HIS . . .	TOUCH HIM
"all that he hath" 1:12	"his bone and flesh" 2:5
POSSESSIONS OF JOB	PERSON OF JOB

2. As Chart G shows, the comparisons of the two trials review chapter 1 and anticipate chapter 2. Mark the phrases in your Bible as you note them.

3. Job's three friends make their appearance in this chapter. Note that "they came every one from his own place" (2:11). The *Berkeley Version* reads, "They met by appointment." *The Living Bible* paraphrases, "They got in touch with each other and traveled from their homes." Review your earlier study of these men (Lesson 2).

II. ANALYSIS

Segment to be analyzed: 2:1-13
Paragraph divisions: at verses 1, 7, 11

A. General Analysis

1. Read the chapter once for general impressions. What similarities to chapter 1 do you observe?

_____

_____

2. Who are the main characters of each paragraph?

_____

_____

_____

3. Describe the attitude, or spirit, behind the words of the following:
(a) Satan (first paragraph)

_____

(b) God (2:3, 6)

_____

(c) Job's wife (2:9)

_____

(d) Job (2:10)

_____

(e) Job's three friends (last paragraph)

_____

B. Paragraph Analysis

1. *Paragraph 2:1-6*

What fact about Satan's activity, stated in chapter 1, is repeated in verses 1-2?

What does God add to this description of Job's spiritual life (1:8)?

Compare 2:5 with 1:11.

2. *Paragraph 2:7-10*

Satan's smiting of Job is reported in such brief, emotionless words that Job's agony of mind and body is hardly perceived. Many Bible expositors identify his loathsome disease as elephantiasis,[1] a severe form of leprosy. Read Deuteronomy 28:27-35 for a similar description. Then check out the following references in the book of Job that reveal some of the horrible aspects of Job's affliction:[2]

(a) insufferable itching of the skin (2:8)
(b) skin cracked and covered with boils, first hard and encrusted, and then festering with worms or maggots (7:5)
(c) foul breath (19:17)
(d) blackened and chapped appearance of the body (30:30)
(e) pain of the limbs (30:17, 30)
(f) extreme emaciation (19:20; 30:18)
(g) anguished frame, made restless by nightly dreams, gasping, and tortures (7:4, 13-15)

What do you think Job's wife really meant by the words "Curse God, and die" (2:9)?

Compare this with Satan's prediction of verse 5. Did she sympathize with Job?

---

1. The disease is so named because the affected skin resembles an elephant's hide.
2. See John Peter Lange, "Job," in *Commentary on the Holy Scriptures*, p. 303.

Was her counsel becoming to her, in view of Job's first words of reply (2:10a)?

What was Job's basic attitude toward his relationship to God, according to 2:10b?

(Note: read the word "evil" as "misfortune" or "adversity.") E. Heavenor writes, "He bows before the sovereign hand of God whether it bestows or takes away, whether it caresses or strikes."[3]

3. Paragraph 2:11-13

Read 7:3. On the basis of this verse is it correct to conclude that some months transpired between the first day of Job's bodily affliction and the arrival of his three friends?

Was Job's condition worse than his three friends had expected to see? Support your answer.

How intense was their mourning?

Account for their week-long silence. Compare this mourning with mourning for the dead (e.g., Gen. 50:10; 1 Sam. 31:13). Do you think Job preferred that his friends speak or keep silent?

For what are the friends to be commended?

III. NOTES

1. *"He sat down among the ashes"* (2:8). This was the garbage dump outside the town, where fires were always burning. It is the saddest picture of Job, showing him as an outcast from the home

3. E. Heavenor, "Job," in *The New Bible Commentary*, ed. F. Davidson, p. 389.

and community that were dear to his heart. "There, in this place of discarded things, sat the man who once had been *the greatest of all the men of the east*."[4]

2. *"One of the foolish women"* (2:10). In this passage, the word "foolish" refers to spiritual dearth, not mental deficiency (see also Ps. 14:1). Similarly, the word "wise" may refer to spiritual wisdom (see Ps. 19:7).

3. *"Shall we not receive evil?"* (2:10). The verb translated "receive" connotes accepting in meekness and patience, without protest. This meaning is expressed in an ancient Canaanite proverb: "If ants are smitten, they do not receive [it passively] but they bite the hand of the man who smites them."[5] NASB translates "receive" as "accept."

IV. FOR THOUGHT AND DISCUSSION

1. Does all suffering experienced by believers originate as Job's did?

2. Explain what each passage teaches about suffering:
   (a) John 9:1-3
   (b) 1 Peter 4:12-14
   (c) Psalm 66:10
   (d) Philippians 3:8
   (e) Hebrews 2:18; 5:8
   (f) 1 Peter 2:21
   (g) 1 Peter 3:18
   (h) 1 Peter 5:10

3. Consider the sufferings of Christ (Luke 24:26; Acts 17:3; Heb. 2:18; 5:8; 13:12; 1 Pet. 4:1).

4. Could Christ have redeemed man without the experience of suffering? Explain the following statement: The blackest hour of history was also its brightest one.

5. Explain the relationship between Christ's suffering and the believer's suffering (2 Cor. 1:5-7; Phil. 3:10-11; 1 Pet. 2:21-23; 4:13; 5:1).

6. How did Job's attitude demonstrate the prayer "Thy will be done"? Have you prayed this prayer with such selflessness?

7. Satan was able to seduce Adam, who had never sinned, yet he was not triumphant over Job, who knew sin. What does this reveal about the power of God's grace in the heart of a sinner?

4. Ibid.
5. As quoted in *The Wycliffe Bible Commentary*, p. 464.

A little boy came to his father one day and asked, "Dad, is Satan bigger than I am?"

"Yes, my boy," said the father.

"Is he bigger than you, Dad?"

"Yes, he's bigger than your dad."

The boy looked surprised but thought again and asked, "Is he bigger than Jesus?"

"No, my boy," answered the father. "Jesus is bigger than he is."

The little fellow smiled as he turned to go his way, and he spoke these words with a conviction that few adults can match, *"Then I am not afraid of him."*

V. FURTHER STUDY

1. You may want to extend your study about Satan to inquire into his origin and his ultimate destiny. Regarding his origin, refer to such passages as John 8:44; 1 John 3:8; 1 Timothy 3:6; Isaiah 14:12-17; Ezekiel 28:12-15.[6] Consult a Bible dictionary and theology textbook for help. On Satan's ultimate destiny, see Revelation 20:1-3; 7:10.

2. Explain how you would answer the following challenge from an unbeliever concerning the problem of pain:

> If God were good, He would wish to make His creatures perfectly happy, and if God were almighty He would be able to do what He wished. But the creatures are not happy. Therefore God lacks either goodness, or power, or both.[7]

VI. WORDS TO PONDER

Remember that it is usually those who have patiently endured to whom we accord the word "blessed." You have heard of Job's patient endurance and how God dealt with him in the end, and therefore you have seen that the Lord is merciful and full of understanding pity for us men (James 5:11, Phillips[8]).

---

6. Some expositors apply the latter two prophecies to the earthly kings of Babylon and Tyre only. See the article "Satan," by D. Edmond Hiebert, in *The Zondervan Pictorial Bible Dictionary*, ed. Merrill C. Tenney, pp. 155-56.

7. See C. S. Lewis, *The Problem of Pain*, pp. 14ff., for answers to this challenge.

8. *New Testament in Modern English.*

Lesson 5
Job Despairs

Job endured agonizing affliction for a time, but eventually he reached his breaking point. When the ravaging disease first touched his body, he may have hoped for a quick recovery. But the relentless, throbbing pain persisted day after day, week after week, month after month (7:3), so that Job cursed the very day of his birth. The chapter discussed in this lesson clearly reveals the awful intensity of his affliction. It is not difficult to sympathize with Job.

I. PREPARATION FOR STUDY

1. Recall from the last lesson that Job's three friends sat with him for a full week without saying a word. Does 4:2 suggest a reason for this? According to 3:1, who broke the silence? What do you think this discloses about Job and about his friends?

_____

_____

_____

2. How is man's body related to his nonphysical part (mind and spirit)? Can physical sickness bring on mental or spiritual distress?

_____

_____

How do you account for the change in Job's attitude from that of 2:10 to that suggested in 3:1? One writer refers to this change as "Job's startlingly abrupt plunge from patience to deep despondency."[1]

1. Meredith G. Kline, "Job," in *The Wycliffe Bible Commentary*, p. 464.

II. ANALYSIS

Segment to be analyzed: 3:1-26
Stanza divisions[2]: at verses 1, 11, 20

A. General Analysis

1. If you have a version in which chapters 3-42 are arranged as poetry, it is recommended that you use it for the studies that follow.[3] This manual will continue to refer to the King James Version.
2. First mark the three stanza divisions in your Bible. Then read the chapter once for general impressions. What is the tone of Job's words?

_____

3. What is the main subject of each stanza?

_____

_____

_____

Explain how the stanzas differ from each other. Compare your conclusions with this outline:

I. Imprecation[4] 3:1-10	II. Lamentation 3:11-19	III. Confusion 3:20-26

B. Stanza Analysis

1. *Stanza 3:1-10: Imprecation*
Observe the strong word "cursed" in verse 1. What phrases does Job use to curse the day of his birth? Does he use the word "curse" in this stanza? Note that the word "let" is repeated throughout the stanza. How does this set the imprecatory tone of the stanza?

_____

_____

_____

2. A stanza in poetry is the equivalent of a paragraph in prose.
3. As noted earlier, the NASB prints this text of Job in a very clear, line-by-line format. ASV *(American Standard Version)* and RSV *(Revised Standard Version)* do essentially the same thing, but with two columns of text on each page.
4. "Imprecate" means to invoke evil upon. Some psalms are called "imprecatory psalms" (e.g., Psalms 35, 52, 58-59, 69, 83, 109, 137, 140).

What is said about day and about night in verse 3?

What verses expand on "that day"?

What verses expand on "that night"?

In your own words, what is Job saying about the night of his conception and about the day of his birth?

Does Job refer to God in this chapter? If so, in what way?

Be sure to answer this question: Does Job indicate in this stanza why he is cursing that day and that night? If so, what is the reason?

Compare 3:10 and 2:10.

2. Stanza 3:11-19: Lamentation
What clue to the tone of this stanza is furnished by the repeated "why"?

Read verse 11 aloud, recreating its tone by using the repeated phrase, "Why didn't I?" How does the phrase "For then [now] should I have" (v. 13) introduce the remainder of the stanza?

What is Job maintaining in verses 13-19?

Job's thought in the first two stanzas may be summarized as follows:
(a) 3:1-10: I wish I had never been born.
(b) 3:11-19: If I had to be born, I wish I would have died immediately afterward.

3. *Stanza 3:20-26: Confusion*

The opening word of this stanza is its clue. (The word "wherefore" should read "why."[5]) Note that the word is also supplied (in italics) in verse 23. In this stanza Job uses the word to ask for an answer. In verses 11 and 12, however, his "why" expressed a lament. But in this stanza Job is asking a philosophical question about cause. He is confused because he does not know *why* this calamity has befallen him. Earlier, Job had accepted the fact of misfortune (e.g., 1;21; 2:10), although he did not understand God's reasons for sending it. Why does he demand reasons now (chap. 3), whereas he did not do so before (chaps. 1-2)?

What paradox is expressed in 3:20 and 3:23?

One writer comments thus: "The most brilliant light can only mock a man in a dungeon, or a bird in a cage."[6] Here are two possible translations and interpretations of 3:25 for your consideration.

(a) "I greatly feared," past tense (as in KJV). This means that Job is enduring the worst imaginable experience or that Job's faith before calamity was not pure from a taint of doubt.

(b) "The thing that I fear," present tense (as in NASB, RSV), meaning that fear is another aspect of Job's anguish of soul.

Verse 26 is also variously translated. The King James Version reads all the verbs in the past tense. Most modern versions read the verse in the present tense, thus: "And I am not at rest, but turmoil comes" (NASB). *The Living Bible* interprets the verse by this interesting paraphrase: "I was not fat and lazy, yet trouble struck me down." What is your interpretation of the verse?

---

5. Usually the word *wherefore* in the KJV means *why*. Sometimes it has the connotation of *therefore* (e.g., Gen. 38:10).
6. E. Heavenor, "Job," in *The New Bible Commentary*, p. 390.

Since context is an important guide to interpretation, it is always good to know the surrounding "neighbors" of any particular verse. Does the context of verses 20-24 help you to understand what Job means in verses 25 and 26? Contrast the hedge of protection (1:10) and the hedge of confinement (3:23).

III. NOTES

1. *"Cursed his day"* (3:1). This means "cursed the day of his birth."

2. *"Raise up their mourning"* (3:8). Most modern versions translate "mourning" as "Leviathan." Magicians (those who "curse the day," 3:8) were thought by many to be able to make this monster perform marvels, such as an eclipse of the sun.

3. *"Why did the knees prevent me?"* (3:12). The word "prevent" should read "receive."

4. *"As an hidden untimely birth"* (3:16). The *New American Standard Bible* translates, "Like a miscarriage which is discarded."

5. *"Before I eat"* (3:24). Various translations of the first line of this verse are suggested. The *New American Standard Bible* reads, "For my groaning comes at the sight of my food."

IV. FOR THOUGHT AND DISCUSSION

1. How would you answer the question of 3:20: "Why is light given to the wretched and life to the bitter soul?" (*Berkeley*). You probably know of Christians, bedridden with pain for years, who have expressed the desire to go to be with their Lord. Why does God sustain life in such a situation? Is there more than one possible answer to such a question?

2. Was Job's physical affliction caused directly by sin in his life? Does he maintain his innocence in the desperate cry of this chapter?

3. In this chapter Job does not curse God, but he does curse his own existence. Since God gave him his life and maintained it by His sovereign will, is Job in effect disputing or doubting God?

4. Does verse 17 teach that there is spiritual peace for the wicked after death? If not, what does it teach?

5. Job's lament is negative throughout. Did you learn any positive spiritual lessons from this chapter?

V. FURTHER STUDY

Refer to a book of theology or doctrine for further study of the following subjects.

1. The relationship between man's body and psyche (soul and spirit).

2. The origin of the individual's personal identity (body-soul-spirit). Scripture teaches that the human race originated in the first man, Adam, and that each person is propagated from him by natural generation (cf. Acts 17:26; Luke 3:23-38). The question is, Does a person's identity (body-soul-spirit) originate at conception, in the mother's womb, or at the moment of birth? Do verses 11-16 suggest an answer? How is the issue of abortion related to this?

VI. WORDS TO PONDER

I can never stop groaning (Job 3:24b, *Today's English Version*).

And even we Christians, although we have the Holy Spirit within us as a foretaste of future glory, also groan to be released from pain and suffering. We, too, wait anxiously for that day when God will give us our full rights as his children, including the new bodies he has promised us—bodies that will never be sick again and will never die (Rom. 8:23, TLB).

Lesson 6

First Cycle of Debate

Chapter 4 is the start of the first of three cycles of debate between Job and his three friends. After Job had broken the week-long silence (chap. 3), his friends one by one spoke out frankly and sometimes harshly, trying to answer his agonized question, "Why?" Job gave reply to each one, telling why he rejected their reasonings.

The following outline of 4:1–31:40 shows the pattern of the three cycles of controversy in the book of Job. (Observe that Eliphaz is the opening speaker of each series, and that Zophar does not speak in the last series.)

			First Cycle			
Eliphaz	chaps.	4-5	➞	Job	chaps.	6-7
Bildad		8	➞	Job		9-10
Zophar		11	➞	Job		12-14
			Second Cycle			
Eliphaz		15	➞	Job		16-17
Bildad		18	➞	Job		19
Zophar		20	➞	Job		21
			Third Cycle			
Eliphaz		22	➞	Job		23-24
Bildad		25	➞	Job		26-31

That such a large space is devoted to human reasonings tells us, among other things, that God does give a hearing to all the thoughts of man.[1]

I. PREPARATION FOR STUDY

1. Review Chart E, observing the context of the passage now under consideration.

---

1. It may be noted here that while the men's diagnoses are wrong or incomplete (38:2; 42:7), much of what they say is true (e.g., 5:8-16).

	King James Version	Substitute Reading
4:6	(entire verse)	Is not your fear of God your confidence, And the integrity of your ways your hope?
17	be more just than God be more pure than his Maker	be just before God be pure before his Maker
19	How much less	How much more (refers to v. 18b)
20-21	(entire verses)	A man may be alive in the morning, but die unnoticed before evening comes. All that he has is taken away; he dies, still lacking wisdom (TEV).
5:6	Although affliction	Affliction (omit "although")
7	Yet man	No! Man (TEV)
24	tabernacle	tent
	not sin	fear no loss
6:3	now	then
	are swallowed up	have been rash
7	(entire verse)	My soul refuses to touch them; They are like loathsome food to me.
10	(entire verse)	This would still be comfort to me; yes, I would leap for joy in unsparing pain, for I have not denied the commands of the Holy one (Berkeley).
13	wisdom	deliverance
14	But	Lest
21	For now ye are nothing	Indeed, you have now become such
29	let it not be iniquity	let there be no injustice
7:20	I have sinned; what shall I do unto thee?	Have I sinned? What have I done to Thee?[2]

2. Consult other modern versions for different renderings of this verse.

2. Recall the descriptions of Job's three friends (see Lesson 2). Become acquainted with these men as *persons* rather than mere *names*, as you begin to study their speeches.

3. The biblical text involved in the next three lessons is exceptionally long. It is recommended that you study each of these lessons in at least three units.

4. Some phrases in the text of the King James Version need clarification. Record the following substitute readings in your Bible.[3] (Other changes will be suggested later in the lesson.)

II. ANALYSIS

Mark in your Bible the stanza divisions shown below. The importance of this cannot be overemphasized.

SPEECH	STANZA DIVISIONS at verses
4:1–5:27	4:1, 7, 12; 5:1, 8, 17
6:1-30	6:1, 8, 14, 24
7:1-21	7:1, 7, 11
8:1-22	8:1, 8, 11
9:1–10:22	9:1, 13, 25; 10:1, 8, 18
11:1-20	11:1, 7, 13
12:1–14:22	12:1, 7, 12; 13:1, 7, 13; 14:1, 7, 13, 18

Chart H is a work sheet. Record on it the main arguments of the speeches of the first cycle. This represents an overview of this phase of the debate. More instructions concerning the work sheet will be given as the lesson progresses.

A. Overview: 4:1–7:21. Eliphaz and Job

1. Read the speech of Eliphaz, in one continuous reading. (chaps. 4-5). Then reread it, stanza by stanza. Record on Chart H a brief summary, in your own words, of the main point of each stanza (examples are given). Then record in the allotted space what you regard as a main point of the speech.

2. Do the same kind of study for Job's answer to Eliphaz (chap. 6) and his words to God (chap. 7).

B. Stanza Analysis: 4:1–7:21

The following questions are suggested to help you analyze each stanza. Let these be starters for more detailed study.

3. The substitute readings are from the NASB, unless otherwise noted.

THE THREE FRIEND'S DIAGNOSES	JOB'S ANSWERS
CHAPS. 4-5	**CHAPS. 6-7**
4:1-6 Don't you fear God?	6:1-7
	8-13
7-11 The innocent don't perish.	14-23
	24-30
12-21	MAIN POINT:
5:1-7	**JOB SPEAKS TO GOD**
8-16	7:1-6
	7-10
17-27	11-21
MAIN POINT:	MAIN POINT:
CHAP. 8	**CHAPS. 9-10**
8:1-7	9:1-12
	13-24
	25-35
8-10	MAIN POINT:
	JOB SPEAKS TO GOD
11-22	10:1-7
	8-17
	18-22
MAIN POINT:	MAIN POINT:
CHAP. 11	**CHAPS. 12-14**
11:1-6	12:1-6
	7-11
	12-25
	13:1-6
7-12	7-12
	13-19
	MAIN POINT:
	JOB SPEAKS TO GOD
13-20	13:20-28
	14:1-6
	7-12
	13-17
	18-22
MAIN POINT:	MAIN POINT:

ELIPHAZ ①

BILDAD ①

ZOPHAR ①

45

1. *Eliphaz Speaks: 4:1–5:27*

(a) 4:1-6. According to 4:2, how was Job affected by his friends' words?

_____

_____

What does 4:3-4 disclose about Job's former ministry with people?

_____

_____

Do you see sarcasm in verse 5?

_____

If not, what may Eliphaz have meant by these words? (In answering this, consider also verse 6.)

_____

_____

(b) 4:7-11. What similar idea is repeated from line to line?

_____

How strong is the word "perish" in this context?

_____

What point is Eliphaz trying to establish here?

_____

(c) 4:12-21. How do verses 12-16 introduce the verses that follow?

_____

_____

Why is the description so lengthy?

_____

How does Eliphaz compare man and God in verses 17-21?

_____

(d) 5:1-7. What kind of person is described in 5:2-5?

_____

Do you think Job might have understood the words to be about him?

_____

What is Eliphaz's philosophy of trouble, according to 5:6-7?

_____

_____

(e) 5:8-16. What is the advice to Job in verse 8?

_____

Compare 5:8 and 5:1.

_____

_____

In what way is God the Dependable Helper, according to 5:9-16?

_____

_____

(f) 5:17-27. In what sense is a person whom God corrects *blessed* (5:17)?

_____

_____

Apply this to Job.

_____

How is the relationship between *blessing* and *chastening* illustrated in verses 18-26? Make a list of the illustrations.

_____

_____

_____

_____

2. *Job Answers Eliphaz: 6:1-30*
As you study, keep in mind that Job is experiencing physical agony throughout this interchange of opinion. It is amazing that he has the strength to speak at all.
(a) 6:1-7. "The arrows of the Almighty are within me" (6:4, NASB). How does this complaint of Job set the tone of this stanza?

_____

_____

What does Job imply about his own experience in verse 5?

_____

(b) 6:8-13. What is Job's frustration, according to these verses?

_____

_____

47

What is Job's testimony regarding his keeping God's command-
ment (6:10, *Berkeley*)?

_____

_____

(c) 6:14-23. What is Job's complaint here?

_____

Observe that he likens his friends to a wadi (KJV, "brook"). There
are hundreds of wadis in Palestine. These are sandy riverbeds that
are flooded in the wet, winter season, but completely dry in the
hot season. Observe the various ways Job develops this illustration
in verses 15-23.

(d) 6:24-30. Job's pleas to his friends are vehement.
List what he says here about
Himself

_____

_____

His friends

_____

_____

What he wants

_____

_____

3. *Job Speaks to God: 7:1-21*
Read verse 17, and note that Job is addressing God. Would you say
that Job is addressing God in verse 12?

_____

In verse 8?

_____

Today's English Version (TEV) begins the address to God at verse
7 with the paraphrase "Remember, God, my life is only wind." Do
the words of 7:1 suggest that Job begins to speak to God in this
verse?

_____

(a) 7:1-6. Does Job make any new lamentations?

_____

(b) 7:7-10. Here Job talks to God about his coming death. Do these verses teach that the soul is annihilated at physical death?

_____

What does Job mean by "Thine eyes will be on me, but I will not be" (7:8*b*, NASB)?

_____

(c) 7:11-21. Explain the meaning of verse 11, in light of verses 7-10.

_____

_____

What is Job's complaint to God in verses 12-19?

_____

Does Job confess to be a sinner, according to 7:20 (KJV or NASB)?

_____

Then what is his problem, according to 7:21?

_____

Is his question of 7:21 based on the assumption that his suffering is a judgment for sin?

_____

C. Summary Questions: 4:1–7:21

1. What is Job's view of life?

_____

_____

2. How does Job view his relation to God?

_____

_____

3. Does Job still recognize God as sovereign over all?

_____

D. Overview: 8:1–10:22. Bildad and Job

1. For a better understanding of the King James text, make the changes listed on the accompanying chart.
2. Survey chapters 8-10 stanza by stanza as you surveyed chapters 4-7. Record your survey on the work sheet (Chart H).

King James Version	Substitute Reading
8:4b (entire line)	Then He recompensed them according to their transgression (Berkeley).
13 hypocrite's	godless man's
18 destroy	pull
21 Till he fill	He will yet fill
9:2 how should man be just with God?	can a man be in the right before God?
13 If	(omit)
21-22 (entire verses)	I am innocent, but I no longer care. I am sick of living. Nothing matters; innocent or guilty, God will destroy us (TEV).
25 post	runner
33 daysman	umpire
34 his fear	dread of Him
35 But it is not so with me	For personally I have no guilty qualms
10:1 I will leave my complaint upon myself	I will give full vent to my complaint
3 despise	reject
7b (entire line)	Yet there is none that can deliver out of thine hand
13 And	Yet
15 yet will I	I dare
15 therefore see thou mine affliction	and conscious of my misery
16 showest thyself marvellous upon me	wouldst show Thy power against me
17 Changes and war are against me	and bring fresh hosts against me (Berkeley)

E. Stanza Analysis: 8:1–10:22

1. *Bildad Speaking: 8:1-22*
(a) 8:1-7. What does Bildad say about God?

_____

_____

How does he account for the tragedy that befell Job's children (8:4)?

_____

_____

What is Bildad's estimate of Job's character, as suggested in 8:6-7?

_____

_____

(b) 8:8-10. This is Bildad's defense of traditionalism. How does he compare the knowledge of one person to the corporate wisdom of past generations?

_____

_____

(c) 8:11-22. How does Bildad describe the godless man's ways and destiny in verses 11-19?

_____

_____

What does he maintain about God's dealings with men of integrity?

_____

_____

2. *Job Answers Bildad: 9:1-35*
(a) 9:1-12. What is Job's description of God in 9:5-12?

_____

_____

In Job's thinking how do these attributes intensify his personal dilemma (9:2-4, 12)?

_____

_____

(b) 9:13-24. What is Job's basic complaint?

_____

Explain how the phrase "multiplieth my wounds without cause" (9:17) represents his festering problem.

_____

_____

(c) 9:25-35. State the grievances contained in the following verses.
25-26

_____

27-31

_____

32-33

_____

34-35

_____

Job cries that there is no mediator ("daysman") between God and himself (9:33). In the context of these verses what does Job believe that a mediator would see in him: his sin, his righteousness, or both?

_____

_____

3. *Job Speaks to God: 10:1-22*
(a) 10:1-7. Observe the tone of bitterness.[4] What does Job claim and charge in verse 7?

_____

_____

(b) 10:8-17. For what does Job magnify God in verses 8-13?[5]

_____

_____

What troubles him, according to verses 14-17?

_____

4. Job had addressed God once in 9:31. From 10:2 on are words Job would speak to God.
5. The similes of 10:10 refer to conception and gestation, and are so represented in the TEV paraphrase: "You gave my father strength to beget me; you made me grow in my mother's womb."

(c) 10:18-22. Compare this stanza with 3:11-19.

_____

_____

F. Summary Questions: 8:1–10:22

1. What is Bildad's explanation of Job's plight?

_____

2. What is Job's reply to Bildad's diagnosis?

_____

G. Overview: 11:1–14:22. Zophar and Job

1. Before reading the passage, note the changes in the King James translation of the text suggested by the full-page chart, for clearer understanding of the meaning.

2. Survey chapters 11-14 stanza by stanza, as you did the earlier chapters. Record your survey on Chart H. Note especially the verse in which Job begins to address God.

H. Stanza Analysis: 11:1–14:22

Now study each stanza in detail, following the procedures used in the earlier part of this lesson. Try to find answers to the following questions.

1. What does Zophar think of Job?

_____

Which of the three friends is most severe with Job?

_____

2. What are your reflections about these words of Zophar? 11:4-5

_____

11:7

_____

11:13-14

_____

King James Version		Substitute Reading
11:3	lies	boasts
6	they are double to that which is	sound wisdom has two sides
7	the Almighty unto perfection	the limits of the Almighty
8	hell	Sheol
12	(entire verse)	And an idiot will become intelligent When the foal of a wild donkey is born a man.
17	age . . . clearer	life . . . brighter
19	make suit unto thee	entreat your favor
12:5	(entire verse)	You have no troubles, and yet you make fun of me; you hit a man who is about to fall (TEV).
10	soul	life
12	With the ancient is wisdom	Wisdom is with aged men
13	With him	With Him (God)
22	discovereth	reveals
23	straiteneth them	leads them away
24	heart	intelligence
13:3	Surely	But
8	accept his person	show partiality for Him
9	Is it good that he should search you out?	Will it be well when He examines you?
11	his dread	dread of Him
27	thou settest a print upon the heels of my feet	setting bounds to my footsteps
28	he, as a rotten thing, consumeth	I am decaying like a rotten thing
14:16b	dost thou not watch over my sin?	and take note of my every sin (Amp. [6])

17	(entire verse)	You bundle them all together
		  as evidence against me (TLB).
		or, You will forgive my sins and put
		  them away;
		You will wipe out all the wrongs
		  I have done (TEV).

6. *Amplified Bible.*

3. In your own words, what is Zophar's diagnosis of Job's plight, and what is his advice?

_____

_____

To what extent is he right, and wrong?

_____

_____

4. What does Job think of Zophar?

_____

In what stanzas does Job especially deride Zophar?

_____

5. What is the force of the word "and" in 12:13 and 12:16?

_____

What does Job say about God's power in 12:12-25?

_____

_____

6. "Though despondency darkens Job's concluding words, it is clear that in this reply to Zophar, his faith has begun its triumphant ascent out of the abyss of despair."[7] Cite examples of this "ascent" from the passage under discussion. For example, what is Job's testimony in 13:15-16?

_____

_____

_____

What is his confidence, according to 13:18?

_____

7. What two requests does Job make of God (13:20-21)?

_____

_____

8. What is Job's question in 13:23?

_____

Compare this with Zophar's charges in 11:2-6.

_____

7. Meredith G. Kline, "Job," in *The Wycliffe Bible Commentary*, p. 472.

9. What is Job's mood in 14:1-12?

10. What high point of yearning does Job reach in 14:13-17?

Compare this with what eventually became assurance in 19:25ff.

11. Does the concluding stanza (14:18-22) show an advance in Job's hope beyond that of the preceding stanza (14:13-17), or is there a retrogression? Can you account for this?

III. FOR THOUGHT AND DISCUSSION

1. Some of Job's words reveal the depths of despondency to which a child of God may fall. What measures can the Christian take to avoid falling into such despair?

2. "Neither is there any daysman [umpire, arbiter, mediator] betwixt us, that might lay his hand upon us both" (9:33). Job was conscious of God's greatness and his own smallness, and his soul cried for firsthand contact with God. "There was no finally satisfactory answer to Job short of the incarnation. The passage is strongly forward-looking to Bethlehem."[8] In what ways is Jesus, as "mediator between God and men" (1 Tim. 2:5), the answer to man's needs?

IV. WORDS TO PONDER

Can you discover the depths of God? (11:7, NASB). If iniquity be in thine hand, put it far away (11:14). Though he slay me, yet will I trust in him (13:15). Man . . . is of few days, and full of trouble (14:1). If a man die, shall he live again? (14:14).

8. E. Heavenor, "Job," in *The New Bible Commentary*, p. 394.

Second Cycle of Debate

Arguments tend to drag on, partly because each person wants to have the last word. Such was the case in the controversies between Job and his three friends. No sooner had the first cycle of debate concluded than each of Job's friends spoke up again, only to be challenged anew by Job. This cycle runs in the following sequence:

Eliphaz	(15)	→	Job (16-17)
Bildad	(18)	→	Job (19)
Zophar	(20)	→	Job (21)

Job's friends were relentless in their charges while his agony continued unabated. No wonder he cried out at one point, "Have pity upon me, have pity upon me, O ye my friends" (19:21).

I. PREPARATION FOR STUDY

1. You may want to continue the study procedure used in Lesson 6. If so, prepare a work sheet similar to Chart H and record brief observations about each stanza in this passage.

2. Mark stanza divisions at the following verses: 15:1, 7, 17; 16:1, 6, 18; 17:1, 3, 6; 18:1, 5; 19:1, 7, 13, 23, 28; 20:1, 12, 20; 21:1, 17, 27.

3. Review the main points of the first cycle of debate that you recorded on Chart H. Try to imagine the feelings between Job and his friends as they launched into a second barrage of words.

4. Record in the text of your King James Version the substitute readings listed in part 1 of the Notes of this lesson.

II. ANALYSIS

As you study this phase of the debate, record on the work sheet (Chart I) the main contention of each speaker. This will help you see the "forest" as you look at all the "trees."

SUMMARY OF SECOND CYCLE OF DEBATE: 15:1—21:34

JOB'S FRIENDS	JOB'S REPLY
ELIPHAZ (chap. 15)	(16-17)
BILDAD (18)	(19)
ZOPHAR (20)	(21)

The selected questions and exercises that follow will direct your attention to the key parts of each speech.

A. Eliphaz: 15:1-35

1. Describe Eliphaz's attitude toward Job as revealed in the opening lines (1-6).

_____

_____

2. What does he charge in verse 13?

_____

3. What do you learn about Job's three friends from 15:9-10?

_____

4. The first line of verse 20 introduces the remainder of the speech. List Eliphaz's descriptions of the wicked man.

_____

_____

B. Job's Reply: 16:1–17:16

1. What is Job's blunt reply in 16:1-3?

_____

Compare 17:10.

_____

2. Compare "I could" (v. 4) with "but I would . . ." (v. 5).

_____

3. What do you observe in this speech about:
(a) Job's agony

_____

(b) Job's testimony of righteousness

_____

(c) Job's waning hope

_____

4. Compare 16:19 and 16:20a. What was Job resting on, according to the words "my advocate is on high"?

_____

In what way is Jesus the perfect advocate? (See Heb. 9:24.)

_____

_____

C. Bildad: 18:1-21

1. What is Bildad's attitude toward Job, according to verses 2-4?

_____

2. Verse 21 summarizes Bildad's speech. List Bildad's dark descriptions of the wicked man in this stanza.

_____

_____

What does he imply by addressing these words to Job?

_____

D. Job's Reply: 19:1-29

1. What does Job say in the opening stanza (19:1-6) about his friends, himself, and God?

_____

_____

2. What is Job's complaint in verses 7-12?

_____

What is so pitiful about his plight described in the next stanza (19:13-22)?

_____

_____

3. Job's flight from the dark valley of 19:13-22 to the mountain peak of 19:23-27 is sudden and glorious. What is the key verse of this peak? Explain how it answers Job's earlier question, "If a man die, shall he live again?" (14:14; cf. 14:1-2).

_____

_____

4. Read 14:13-15 again. Is his conviction about life after death more firm in chapter 19?

5. Job believed that any hope for him beyond this life rested in someone outside himself, someone from heaven. Study the growth of this faith as seen in the following verses:
    (a) "There is no mediator to bring us together" (9:33).
    (b) "My advocate is on high" (16:19, NASB).
    (c) "Lay down a pledge for me with Thyself" (17:3, NASB).
    (d) "I know that my Redeemer lives" (19:25, NASB).

E. Zophar: 20:1-29

Verse 5 introduces Zophar's theme, and verse 29 summarizes it. How does he describe the wicked man?

_____

_____

Compare his charges against Job with Bildad's.

_____

F. Job's Reply: 21:1-34

1. Recall Zophar's words that "the triumphing of the wicked is short, and the joy of the hypocrite but for a moment" (20:5). Most of Job's reply challenges that premise. Observe what Job says in verses 7-16. (Compare the KJV rendering of 21:7 with TLB paraphrase: "The truth is that the wicked live on to a good old age, and become great and powerful.")

2. Read verses 17-21 and 28-33 in a modern paraphrase (e.g., TLB) to grasp what Job is contending here.

3. Job is obviously exaggerating when he implies that *all* wicked men live to a ripe old age, in health and prosperity (cf. 21:7). Explain his real view, as expressed in verses 23-26.

_____

_____

"Some men stay healthy till the day they die; they die happy and at ease, and their bodies are well-nourished. Others have no happiness at all; they live and die with bitter hearts. But all alike die and are buried; they all are covered with worms" (21:23-26, TEV).

4. How does Job conclude this reply (21:34)?

_____

III. NOTES

1. In your analysis use the following substitute readings. (They are taken from the NASB, unless otherwise indicated.)

2. The word "redeemer" in 19:25 translates the Hebrew *go'el* (lit., "kinsman"). The *go'el* was the nearest blood relation, whose duty it was to defend the cause, property, or person of his kinsman, to avenge wrongs done to him, and to acquit him of charges laid against him. Read Hebrews 7:25. Why is Jesus the perfect Kinsman-Redeemer?

King James Version	Substitute Reading
15:12　wink at	flash
15　he . . . saints	He . . . angels
25　strengtheneth himself	conducts himself arrogantly
29　neither shall he prolong the perfection thereof upon the earth	his grain will not bend down to the ground
16:19　my record	my advocate
21　one might plead for a man with God	a man might plead with God
21　for his neighbor	with his neighbor
17:3　who . . . will strike hands with me?	Who . . . will be my guarantor?
16　(entire verse)	Will it go down with me to Sheol? Shall we together go down into the dust?
19:7　judgment	justice
26　in my flesh shall I see God	from the vantage point of my flesh, I shall see God[1]
20:13　spare	desires
21:17　How oft is the candle of the wicked put out!	How often is the lamp of the wicked put out?[2]

IV. FOR THOUGHT AND DISCUSSION

1. What is the Bible's answer to the questions of Eliphaz: "Can any man be really pure? Can anyone be right with God?" (15:14, TEV).

2. Have you met people who act like those described in 15:25 and 21:15? How should believers respond to people who express such scorn and blasphemy?

3. Do you think Job's testimony of 16:17 is true?

4. Do you think Job suffered chiefly on account of physical pain (e.g., 16:7-16) or on account of being rejected by relatives and friends (19:13-22)?

1. See Gleason L. Archer, *A Survey of Old Testament Introduction*, p. 449.
2. The punctuation of this sentence could be a combination of question mark and exclamation point (sometimes called *interrobang*). To the question: "How often?" Job implies this answer: "Not as often as you contend."

5. The scales of justice will be balanced in eternity. Does evil ever find retribution in this life?

6. Have you experienced a long-term trial that made you wonder if God was aware of your plight? Consider the faith that is suggested by these lines:

> Thrice blest is he to whom is given
> The instinct that can tell
> That God is on the field, when He
> Is most invisible.
>
> F. W. Faber

7. What have you learned about comforting others from your study of this lesson?

8. Why must Jesus be Mediator to be Savior?

9. Jesus as Redeemer is the Christian's Kinsman. Why did He have to become a member of the human race (Phil. 2:5-11) in order to redeem souls from the penalty of eternal death (Gal. 4:4-5; Titus 2:14)?

10. Did God love the human race in a less intimate way before Jesus' incarnation? In answering this consider the following comment: "When God became flesh in Jesus He did not come nearer to human nature than He had ever been; but He came into visibility."[3]

V. WORDS TO PONDER

If a man die, shall he live again? (14:14)

D. L. Moody once said: "I don't expect to die, and if you take up a paper and read, 'D. L. Moody is dead,' don't you believe a word of it. . . . I have a building on high that is eternal in the heavens, and I myself have a like eternity."[4]

I know that my redeemer liveth (19:25).

---

3. G. Campbell Morgan, *The Answers of Jesus to Job*, p. 71.
4. Stanley Gundry and Patricia Gundry, eds. and comps., *The Wit and Wisdom of D. L. Moody* (Chicago: Moody, 1974), p. 46.

Lesson 8

Third Cycle of Debate

Job's unrelenting friends renew their arguments and accusations with increasing ferocity. Earlier they had indirectly charged that he was suffering on account of sin. Now they freely say: "It is not because you fear God that he reprimands you and brings you to trial. No, it's because you have sinned so much, and because of all the evil you do" (22:4-5, TEV).

Recall the opening chapters of the book that explain why Job was stricken with a plague of boils. Keep this reason in mind as you study the diagnoses of Job's friends. Also, while reading Job's speeches, recall Satan's prediction that Job would blaspheme God if his body was afflicted: "He will curse thee to thy face" (2:5). Has Job come close to such blasphemy yet?

I. PREPARATION FOR STUDY

1. Scan the chapters and note the speakers along the way. Check your findings with this breakdown:

Eliphaz	(22)		Job	(23-24)
Bildad	(25)	**⟹**	Job	(26-31)

Observe that Zophar is not mentioned in this cycle.[1]

2. Note the length of Job's last speech (six chapters). Contrast this with Bildad's short speech (25:1-6). How do the opening phrases of 27:1 and 29:1 help to unify chapters 26-31 into one speech?[2]

---

1. Some hold that Zophar is the speaker in 27:13-23. (See E. Heavenor, "Job," in *The New Bible Commentary*, p. 402.)
2. Some assign portions of these chapters (e.g., 27:13-23 and chap. 28) to other speakers or understand them as later speeches of Job.

3. What is the last sentence in 31:40? How does it conclude the three cycles of debates between Job and his friends?

_____

_____

_____

Review Chart E that shows the sequence of the three cycles.
4. Mark stanza divisions in your Bible at the following verses: 22:1, 12, 21; 23:1, 8; 24:1, 13, 18; 25:1; 26:1, 5; 27:1, 7, 13; 28:1, 12, 23; 29:1, 15, 21; 30:1, 9, 16, 24; 31:1, 5, 9, 13, 16, 24, 29, 38.

II. ANALYSIS (See III. NOTES)

Chart J is a work sheet. Record on it the main points of each speech in the third cycle. Make these entries as you proceed with your study of this lesson. (Review the entries you made on the similar work sheet of Chart I.)

A. Eliphaz: 22:1-30

1. What are some of Eliphaz's strong charges of 22:5-9?

_____

_____

Do you think the charges are true? Compare Job's words of 29:11-17.

_____

_____

_____

2. What is the counsel of Eliphaz in 22:21-30?

_____

What does he imply about Job?

_____

_____

3. What do you think was Eliphaz's concept of the grace of God?

_____

_____

65

JOB'S FRIENDS	JOB'S REPLIES
ELIPHAZ (chap. 22)	(23-24)
BILDAD (25)	(26)
	(27)
	(28)
	(29)
	(30)
	(31)

B. Job's Reply: 23:1–24:25

1. Study chapter 23 to learn what it reveals about:
    (a) Job's persistence in searching for the answer to his plight.
    (b) Job's conviction about his own innocence.
    (c) Job's underlying trust in God.
2. Compare 23:3 with 22:21 and 42:5.

_____

_____

How is John 14:8-11 related to this?

_____

_____

3. Compare 23:8-9 and 23:10. Note the pivotal word "but."

_____

_____

4. What does chapter 24 teach about:
    (a) The ways of wicked men (24:1-17).
    (b) The judgments of wicked men (24:18-25).

C. Bildad: 25:1-6

Bildad speaks only a few final words. He adds no new argument to what has been said previously (cf. 4:7-9; 15:14 ff.; 9:2; 14:4). Bildad simply wants to underscore what he sees as the crucial issue of Job's problem. What is his point? Had Job claimed sinless perfection for himself? Why is it that Bildad's statements, true as they are, fail to help Job?

_____

_____

D. Job's Reply and Concluding Remarks: 26:1–31:40

Chapter 26 is Job's reply to what Bildad has just said (chap. 25). After making this reply, Job apparently waits for Zophar to speak, since he was the third speaker in the earlier rounds. Zophar apparently chooses not to say anything, whereupon Job takes the opportunity to address the three men as a group. These additional remarks are introduced at two places by the phrase "Moreover Job continued his parable" (27:1; 29:1).

67

1. *Chapter 26*
Observe the sarcasm of 26:2-4. What is Job's main point in verses 5-14?

_____

_____

How does his description of God's work in creating and sustaining the universe compare with Bildad's (25:1-5)?

_____

Try to state verse 14 in your own words.

_____

_____

2. *Chapter 27*
Observe the bright words of testimony in verses 2-6. What do they reveal about Job's heart at this time?

_____

Explain how verse 8 represents the theme of the second stanza (27:7-12).

_____

_____

What do verses 13-23 describe?

_____

_____

Compare verse 13 with Zophar's words of 20:29.

_____

F. Delitzsch comments:

> In the following strophe Job now begins as Zophar (ch xx.29) concluded. He gives back to the friends the doctrine they have fully imparted to him. They have held the lot of the evil-doer before him as a mirror, that he may behold himself in it and be astounded; he holds it before them, that they may perceive how not only his bearing under suffering, but also the form of the affliction, is of a totally different kind.[3]

3. F. Delitzsch, *The Book of Job*, p. 72.

3. Chapter 28

This is one of the classic chapters in the Bible on wisdom. Can you explain how Job was able to express such a calm and beautiful meditation at such a trying time?

_____

_____

Analyze this chapter using the following outline and keys:

> Treasures Discoverable by Man (28:1-11)
>> "There is . . . a place for gold," 28:1.
> Wisdom Not Discoverable by Unaided Man (28:12-22)
>> "Where is the place of understanding?" 28:12
> Only God Knows the Place of Wisdom (28:23-28)
>> "He knoweth the place thereof," 28:23.

Observe the description in 28:1-11 of mining precious metals. See _Today's English Version_ for a clear rendering of this stanza. In view of 28:12, what is Job's main point in 28:1-11?

_____

_____

Observe the negative statements in 28:12-22. What is Job's point?

_____

_____

How does the last stanza (28:23-28) answer the question posed in the previous stanza?

_____

_____

Compare verse 23 and verse 28.

_____

_____

4. Chapters 29-30

This part of Job's "parable" has two main divisions, as shown on Chart K. List some of Job's descriptions of his past experiences and ministries (29:1-25) and of his present woes (30:1-31). What are the first two words of verses 1, 9, and 16 in chapter 30?

_____

_____

(Underline these and 29:2 in your Bible.)

PAST BLESSINGS (chap. 29)	PRESENT WOES (chap. 30)
"in months past" (29:2)	"but now" (30:1)
29:1	30:1 SOCIAL PERSECUTION BY PEOPLE
	30:16 PHYSICAL PERSECUTION BY GOD
29:25	30:31

Observe the many occurrences of the pronouns "I," "my," and "me" in chapter 29. Do you detect anything of self-righteousness here?

5. Chapter 31
This speech of Job, the last in the three cycles of debate, is the climax of his protestation of innocence. He speaks about (1) his personal life (31:1-12); (2) his relationships with his neighbor (31:13-23); and (3) his relationship with God (31:24-40). The key repeated word of the speech is "if." Read the chapter and count the many occurrences of the word. What is Job's method of protesting his innocence?

Identify the verses in which Job disclaims the following sins:

70

Sin	Verse
Immorality	
Thoughtlessness	
Idolatry	
Bitterness toward enemies	
Insincerity	

What is Job's plea in verse 35?

_____

_____

(See III. Notes for a substitute reading of verse 35*b*.)

* * *

"The words of Job are ended" (31:40). This concluding statement is short but full of force. "He had nothing more to say. The mystery was unsolved, and he relapsed into silence..."[4] Only briefly, toward the book's conclusion, does Job speak again (40:3-5; 42:1-6). Those crucial words are his response to the voice of God. We must withhold our final verdict concerning Job until we have studied those concluding chapters.

III. NOTES

Mark the accompanying substitute readings (from NASB) in your Bible before you begin your analysis.

IV. FOR THOUGHT AND DISCUSSION

1. Apply 22:21-30 to modern Christian living.
2. Man can know God only if God reveals Himself to man. Why? Read John 14:9. In what sense is Jesus the revelation of God the Father?
3. Have you experienced the truth of 23:10?
4. Read Job 23:14. In what ways does the doctrine of the sovereignty of God encourage Christians?
5. What is the awesome truth in the phrase "No man is sure of life" (24:22)? Does this apply to all people of all times?

4. G. Campbell Morgan, *The Book of Job*, p. 182.

King James Version		Substitute Reading
22:4	for fear of thee	because of your reverence
15	Hast thou marked the old way?	Will you keep to the ancient path?
21	him	Him
23	thou shalt put away	if you remove
29	men	you
29	thou shalt say, there is lifting up	you will speak with confidence
30a	the island of the innocent	one who is not innocent
30b	(entire line)	and help even sinners by your pure hands (TLB)
23:13	in one mind	unique
17	because I was not cut off before	but I am not silenced by
25:2	him	Him
26:2a	(entire line)	What a help you are to the weak!
6	Hell	Sheol
28:3	He setteth an end to darkness	Men explore the deepest darkness (TEV)
30:11	he	He
31:35b	and that mine adversary had written a book	and the indictment which my adversary has written

6. The one who counsels people experiencing trial should also comfort them. Why? How does the Holy Spirit minister as both Counselor and Comforter?

7. Bildad's last words (chap. 25) are fatalistic and without hope. How do God's love and the cross of Calvary shed light on such hopelessness?

8. Who takes the initiative in the conversion of a soul—the person himself or God? Is this always the case? Justify your answer.

9. Read what Proverbs 8-9 record about wisdom. Who is the truly wise man?

10. Job was a man of many good works (chap. 29). What is the place of good works in the daily walk of a Christian?

11. Job feared that God was a judge who was uninterested in his plight (31:35) and unfair in this neglect. How do you look upon God as your judge? Refer to Hebrews 12:12-24 as you think about this.

V. WORDS TO PONDER

God's testimony about Himself:

> And there is no other God besides me,
> A righteous God and a Savior;
> There is none except me (Isa. 45:21*b*, NASB).

Job's testimony about God:

> But he knoweth the way that I take: When he hath tried me, I shall come forth as gold (Job 23:10).

> It is a great thing for the human soul when it ceases to listen to the opinion of neighbours, and the arguments of philosophers, and the futilities of the clever men of earth, and flings itself out into the clear light of the judgments and findings of God.
> When any soul does that, it finds there Jesus the Mediator of a new covenant, whose blood makes possible the activity of mercy upon the basis of the strictest justice. Before the Throne, through the mediation of the Mediator, justice and mercy meet together, righteousness and peace kiss each other.[5]

5. G. Campbell Morgan, *The Answers of Jesus to Job*, pp. 99-100.

Lesson 9

Job 32:1–34:37

Elihu's First Two Speeches

After Job replied to their charges, his friends spoke no more; their cause seemed hopeless. A younger man, Elihu, had been listening to the debate but had not interrupted out of courtesy. Since they had no more to say, and Job had finished his part, Elihu unloaded the burden of his heart.

Six chapters of Job are devoted to Elihu's speeches.[1] We shall learn in this lesson and those following that Elihu's diagnosis of Job's plight was more correct than that of the three friends, although it too was deficient. Chart L shows the important place occupied by Elihu's speeches in the book of Job. Observe the progression.

THE CONTEXT OF ELIHU'S SPEECHES

Chart L

1	4	32	38 42
THE PROBLEM OF PAIN	THE INCORRECT ANSWERS OF THE THREE FRIENDS	AN ENLIGHTENED ANSWER	GOD'S PERFECT ANSWER
JOB	ELIPHAZ, ZOPHAR, BILDAD	ELIHU	GOD

1. The word "speeches" in 33:1 of the KJV is translated as singular "speech" in most versions. It cannot be determined how long Elihu may have paused in his discourse at 34:1, 35:1, and 36:1. (Read the verses.) If the six chapters constitute one speech, it may still be said that there were four main parts of the speech. For easier reference in this lesson we are referring to Elihu's words as "speeches."

74

I. PREPARATION FOR STUDY

1. Recall your brief introduction to Elihu in Lesson 2 (IV. D.). There it was pointed out that the name Elihu means literally "He is my God," or "my God is He." Compare this with the Jewish name *Elijah* ("my God is Jehovah"). What else do you know about this man?

2. What had Job's three friends tried to persuade him to admit, throughout the controversy of chapters 4-31?

_____

What was Job's response?

_____

_____

Answers to these two questions form the background for Elihu's entrance into the dialogue.

3. Keep in mind as you study Elihu's speeches that he, like Job and his three friends, was not aware of Satan's meeting with God out of which Job's calamities originated.

4. Chart M shows the structural arrangement of chapters 32-37. Study it carefully at this time. Keep this overview in mind while you analyze each speech. Observe on the chart that the first three speeches stem from statements of Job that Elihu quotes. The fourth and final speech gives Elihu's philosophy of the place of suffering and the power of God.

5. Mark in your Bible the substitute readings for chapters 32-37, as shown in III. NOTES.

II. ANALYSIS

Segments to be analyzed: 32:1–33:33 (first speech); 34:1-37 (second speech)
Stanza divisions: at verses 32:1, 6, 11, 15; 33:1, 8, 12, 19, 29, 31; 34:1, 10, 16, 21, 31

A. Setting: 32:1-5

This is our introduction to Elihu. What phrase describing Elihu's feelings is repeated four times?

_____

Why was Elihu angry with Job?

_____

THE SPEECHES OF ELIHU

32:1	32:6	33:1	34:1	35:1	36:1	37:1

ELIHU'S ANSWERS TO JOB / ELIHU'S PHILOSOPHY

FIRST SPEECH	SECOND SPEECH	THIRD SPEECH	FOURTH SPEECH

INTRODUCTION	FIRST QUOTE		SECOND AND THIRD QUOTES			GOD AND MEN	GOD AND NATURE

32:15	33:8	33:12	34:1	34:10	35:1	36:1	36:22

THREE FRIENDS ADDRESSED	JOB ADDRESSED	ELIHU QUOTES JOB	ELIHU'S RESPONSE TO FIRST QUOTE	ELIHU QUOTES JOB	ELIHU'S RESPONSE TO SECOND QUOTE	ELIHU'S RESPONSE TO THIRD QUOTE	PLACE of SUFFERING	POWER of GOD

SETTING			GOD'S GRACE		GOD'S RIGHTEOUSNESS		GOD'S POWER

lesson 9	lesson 10

76

Why was he indignant regarding the three friends?

_____

INTRODUCTION		DIAGNOSIS	
ELIHU SALUTES THE THREE FRIENDS	ELIHU SALUTES JOB	ELIHU QUOTES JOB	ELIHU CHALLENGES JOB'S STATEMENTS
32:6	32:15	33:8	33:12 33:33

B. Elihu's First Speech: 32:6–33:33

Chart N shows the main parts of Elihu's first speech. Observe the long introduction.

1. *Introduction: 32:6–33:7*
(a) Elihu Salutes the Three Friends: 32:6-14
Observe Elihu's courtesy in verses 6-7. Note also his honesty in rejecting the formula that age equals wisdom (32:8-10). Elihu's frankness shows up in the next stanza (32:11-14). What is his appraisal of the three friends' diagnosis?

_____

(b) Elihu Salutes Job: 32:15-33:7
What does Elihu say about:
(1) The three friends

_____

(2) His own heart

_____

(3) His passion to speak

_____

(4) His motivation in speaking

_____

Observe that Elihu addresses Job by name five times: 34:5, 7, 35, 36; 35:16. Did any of the three friends do this?

2. *Diagnosis: 33:8-33*
This is the core of Elihu's first speech. Observe on Chart N that the first three speeches answer specific statements made by Job.[2]
(a) Elihu Quotes Job: 33:8-11.
What two statements had Job made in his speeches, according to this passage?

Compare 13:24, 27 and 33:10-11 for exact quotes. Do you recall Job's protestations of innocence in words at least similar to 33:9-11? Read 10:7; 12:4; 16:17; 23:12; 27:5-6; 29:14. Had Job ever complained that God was against him?

Recall that Job had confessed iniquity in the course of his speeches (e.g., 7:21 and 13:26). How do you explain this apparent inconsistency?

(b) Elihu Challenges Job's Statements: 33:12-33
Elihu's reaction to Job's plaint was, "You are not right in this" (33:12, NASB). As you study verses 12-33 note especially references to Job's sinfulness and to God's graciousness toward Job. Elihu refers to God as one who *speaks* and as one who *corrects.* Pursue this further, recording your observations on the work sheet (Chart O).
How does Elihu end his speech?

2. Most of Elihu's quotes of Job are not word for word but are paraphrases of what he meant to say.

C. Elihu's Second Speech: 34:1-37

Since Elihu has invited Job to reply to his comments (33:32), he apparently pauses now, waiting. But Job is silent, and Elihu continues to speak. The structure of the second speech is similar to that of the first: introductory call to hear (34:2-4); indirect quotations from Job's earlier speeches (34:5-9); Elihu's answers (34:10-30); and concluding remarks (34:31-37). Organizing your study around this outline. The following selected questions concern the key parts of this speech.

ELIHU CHALLENGES JOB: 33:12-33   Chart O

	HOW	WHY
GOD SPEAKS 33:12-18		
GOD CORRECTS 33:19-28		
SUMMARY 33:29-30		
CONCLUSION 33:31-33		

1. In 34:5-6 what does Elihu quote Job as having said?

_____

(Elihu responds to this in verses 7-8 and 10-37.) Make the following comparisons:

Job's Statements	Elihu's Indirect Quotes
27:6	34:5a
27:2	34:5b
16:12-17	34:6

79

2. In 34:9 what does Elihu quote Job as having said?

_____

(Elihu's response is reported in chapter 35. See Chart M, p. 76.)
3. Elihu's main contention in the second speech is that Almighty God never perverts justice (34:12). What are some of the points he makes in 34:10-30 to support and illustrate this?

_____

4. What biting remarks does Elihu make about Job in 34:35-37?

_____

_____

_____

III. NOTES

Mark these substitute readings (from NASB) in your Bible before you begin your analysis.

	King James Version	Substitute Reading
33:6	I am according to thy wish in God's stead	I belong to God like you
7	my terror shall not	no fear of me should
10	he findeth occasions	He invents pretexts
12	that God	for God
13	Why dost thou strive against him? for	Why do you complain against Him, that
17	hide pride from man	keep man from pride
19	He is chastened	Man is . . . chastened
23	If there be a messenger with him, an interpreter	If there is an angel as mediator for him
34:4	judgment	what is right
6	my wound is incurable without transgression	My wound in incurable, though I am without transgression
31	Surely it is meet to be said unto God	It is well to confess to God (Berkeley)

IV. FOR THOUGHT AND DISCUSSION

1. Is wisdom related to age and experience? Discuss Elihu's statement "It is not growing old that makes men wise" (32:9, TEV).

2. Can you think of any New Testament exhortations to respect the counsel of older folk?

3. In what various ways does God speak to people, saved and unsaved? Do people always hear Him (33:14)? Read Hebrews 1:1-3 and observe how the phrase "God hath spoken" is woven throughout the long sentence.

4. What are the good fruits of God's chastising His children (cf. 33:19-30)?

5. Many people reject the teaching of 34:12 and accuse God of injustice and coldness for allowing catastrophes such as the drowning of an entire village by a tidal wave. What are your thoughts about this?

6. What is genuine confession of sin? What is the place of such confession in the life of a Christian?

V. WORDS TO PONDER

> God does all this again and again;
>   he saves the life of a person,
> and gives him the job of living.
>   (Job 33:29-30, TEV)

Job 35:1–37:24

Elihu's
Concluding Speeches

Elihu was vehement and severe in his first two speeches, charging Job with rebellion. His two concluding speeches, to be studied in this lesson, are just as devastating, as the wrath that was kindled in his heart keeps bursting forth. It is impossible to imagine the mental torture that the speeches must inflict on Job, who is still enduring physical agony. Our studies in these chapters of the book of Job reveal among other things how desperately man, even redeemed man, needs to hear the sure and true voice of God. In the drama of Job, that voice sounds forth after Elihu falls silent (Lesson 11).

I. PREPARATION FOR STUDY

1. Chart P gives a general survey of Elihu's third and fourth speeches. Keep it in mind as you study this lesson.

ELIHU'S THIRD AND FOURTH SPEECHES: 35:1—37:24   Chart P

35:1	36:1		36:22	37:24
THIRD SPEECH	**FOURTH SPEECH**			
	GOD AND MEN		GOD AND NATURE	
ELIHU'S RESPONSE TO JOB'S THIRD STATEMENT (34:9)	THE PLACE OF SUFFERING		THE POWER OF GOD	
GOD'S RIGHTEOUSNESS			GOD'S POWER	

2. Elihu's third speech (chap. 35) is his response to a statement of Job quoted in 34:9. Read the verse again and review its place in the larger context of Chart M.

II. ANALYSIS

Segments to be analyzed: 35:1-16 (third speech); 36:1–37:24 (fourth speech)
Stanza divisions: at verses 35:1, 4, 9; 36:1, 17, 22; 37:1, 14, 21

A. Elihu's Third Speech: 35:1-16

1. *Elihu Quotes Job: 35:1-3*
Observe how Elihu restates Job's words in 35:3, which he had summarized in 34:9. What other quote is added?

Read the following passages in which Job had indirectly made the complaint expressed in 35:3*b*: 9:22; 10:3; 21:7ff. Also compare 21:15, in which Job describes the position taken by ungodly men.

2. *Elihu Answers Job: 35:4-8; 35:9-16*
(Note: you will find it helpful to read these two stanzas in a modern paraphrase.)
   Elihu now answers the two questions posed in 35:3. In 35:4-8 he maintains that God is not affected by man's actions, for He is the transcendent God, whose throne is higher than the heavens. (Compare the words of Eliphaz, 22:1-3.) Do you agree with this? Did Job think that God is affected by man's actions (see 7:17-21)?
   Elihu answers the second question in 35:9-16. He implies that Job does not experience the blessing (profit) he desires because he prays from a heart of vanity. What two kinds of prayers are described in this stanza?
   Here is *The Living Bible*'s paraphrase of the last three verses of chapter 35:

> And it is even more false to say that he [God] doesn't see what is going on. He **does** bring about justice at last, if you will only wait. But do you cry out against him because he does not instantly respond in anger? Job, you have spoken like a fool.

B. Elihu's Fourth Speech: 36:1–37:24

Elihu is at his best in this final speech. He concentrates on God as the ultimate answer to man's problem of pain. "Around God is awesome majesty. . . . He is exalted in power; and He will not do violence to justice and abundant righteousness" (37:22-23, NASB). This is the true answer to Job's problem, as we shall learn from the words of the Lord in the next chapters. thus Elihu is the forerunner of the Lord in this drama of Job.

Chart Q is a partially completed analytical chart, showing the structure of Elihu's speech. Use it as a work sheet to record your observations. (Mark in your Bible the small stanza divisions shown, in addition to the ones given earlier in the lesson.) Study the various outlines and fill in the blanks.

1. What is Elihu's point in each stanza?

2. In your own words, what is Elihu's philosophy of suffering (36:3-21)?

3. In the section called "Majestic Sovereignty of the Afflicter," on Chart Q, note such key phrases as "We know him not" (36:26) and "O Job . . . dost thou know?" (37:14-15).

4. Observe the prominence of storm in the illustrations from nature. Who controls the storm's course and its giving way to fair weather?

How appropriate were these illustrations in view of Job's plight?

5. In what way are the sovereign majesty and power of God related to the problem of human affliction?

How does Elihu make the connection?

Consider the following comment:

> The intimate relation thus suggested between God's rule of nature and his rule of history prepares for Elihu's concluding application to Job. If man cannot comprehend God's natural rule, he ought not expect to comprehend God's moral rule.[1]

1. Meredith G. Kline, "Job," in *The Wycliffe Bible Commentary*, p. 486.

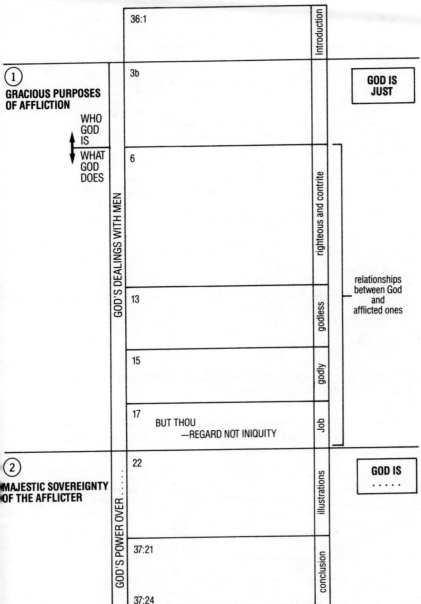

6. Recall again how Job's afflictions first came upon him (chaps. 1-2). As you consider everything Elihu has said in these speeches, how do you appraise his contribution to the discussion?

_____

_____

Does he charge that sin is the *cause* of Job's suffering or the *outcome* of it?

_____

Does he accuse Job of being unteachable under the instructive disciplines of God?

_____

Point out the strengths and weaknesses in Elihu's comments.

_____

_____

7. If you were Job, what questions would you still have after hearing Elihu?

_____

_____

III. NOTES

Mark these substitute readings (from the NASB) in your Bible before you begin your analysis:

King James Version		Substitute Reading
35:3	thee	You (note capitalized Y)
8	(entire verse)	Your sins may hurt another man, or your good deeds may profit him (TLB)
36:6	right	justice
9	exceeded	magnified themselves
29	noise	thundering
30	light	lightning
37:10	straitened	frozen
24	wise of heart	conceited (Berkeley)

IV. FOR THOUGHT AND DISCUSSION

1. God is both transcendent (above and beyond) and immanent (within and around). Apply this description of Him to John 3:16. What kind of being would God be if He were only transcendent? What kind of being would He be if He were only immanent? When man suffers, does God perform as both the transcendent and the immanent one?

2. Is God grieved by every sin of man? How sinful is the "smallest" of sins? (Cf. Rom. 7:13.) A Christian once remarked that "the tiniest sin that settled on his soul gave God as much pain as the speck of grit blown into his own eye." Why is confession of sin to God so important for Christians (see 1 John 1:9)?

3. Is there "profit" in living righteously? If so, what is it? And how is the profit appropriated personally?

4. What are some reasons a Christian should live righteously? What should be the grand motivation?

5. How does the strict discipline of an athlete illustrate some of the purposes of trials from God?

6. "An upright man's prayer, when it keeps at work, is very powerful" (James 5:16, Williams[2]). Why is the effectiveness of prayer directly related to the heart of the person who prays?

7. What can a person learn about God from such natural phenomena as rain, thunder, lightning, snow, cold, and heat? (Cf. Rom. 1:19-20.) What can one learn about God and about himself from the experience of physical affliction? Why did Christ experience *physical* death?

8. Elihu was the last of Job's human counselors. Do you think he was a good counselor? How can Christians counsel sick people effectively? What are the essential things that should be shared in word and spirit?

* * *

Thus concludes the longest section in the book of Job (34 chapters). It contains the self-vindications of Job and the judgments of his four companions (4:1–37:24). Many mistaken views are expressed throughout the book. Satan was wrong in charging that Job served God for what he could get. What were the mistaken views of the following?

---

2. Charles B. Williams, *New Testament in the Language of the People* (Chicago: Moody, 1972).

Job's wife

_____

_____

Job's three friends

_____

_____

Elihu

_____

_____

Job

_____

_____

Of Job's four acquaintances, Elihu came closest to the truth, so that his speeches prepared the way for the next voice to be heard, the Lord's:

> His ministry accomplished, Elihu retires from the scene. He has prepared the way of the Lord in the hearts of Job and his friends. From the literary perspective, the Elihu discourse forms an eminently successful transition to the following theophany [ch. 38 ff.].[3]

V. WORDS TO PONDER

> Behold, God is great, and we know him not (Job 36:26).
> No man hath seen God at any time (John 1:18).
> He that hath seen me hath seen the Father (John 14:9).
> That they may know thee the only true God (John 14:3).

3. Kline, p. 486.

The Lord Speaks to Job

The men are in deadlock; God finally breaks His silence with words directed to Job. This servant of God had long wished for a personal interview with his Lord (cf. 13:22; 23:3; 31:35), and now the moment has arrived. It is interesting to note that Job, who had much to say to his friends, speaks only briefly to God. Our study of this lesson will reveal the reason for this.

Job's desire to hear Him is not God's sole reason for speaking. God speaks because the full truth that His children need to hear has not yet been delivered. So far Job had heard only the reasonings of his friends plus his own troubled thoughts about his affliction. And all of this added up to utter confusion. Then it was that "the Lord answered Job out of the whirlwind" (38:1). Divine revelation, not human reasoning, is the only solution to the dilemma of man. This was true in the first days of man's history, and it stands true today.

Man can know God fully only through divine revelation (see diagram). Human reasoning cannot pierce the barrier, because it is defiled and restricted by sin. Divine revelation answers the primary question, "How can a man be saved?" It also answers related questions such as the one that tormented Job, "Why do godly people suffer in this life?"

Perhaps Job's physical pain even subsided while the Lord was speaking.

I. PREPARATION FOR STUDY

1. It is well to pause at this point in the drama of Job, to understand better why God chose to speak at this time and why He said what He said. Sharpen your perspective by recalling the following.

(a) Job was a righteous man, one who worshiped God and was faithful to Him (1:1-5).

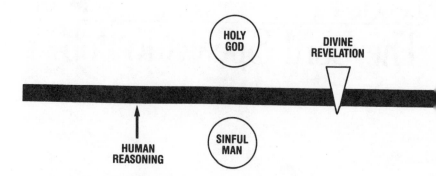

(b) God initiated the action of this drama when He commended Job in the presence of Satan (1:8).

(c) Satan challenged God to test Job's righteousness by painful affliction (1:11; 2:5).

(d) God accepted the challenge by sending affliction, to show the integrity of Job's heart (1:12; 2:6).

(e) Job was not aware of the encounter between Satan and God.

(f) Job's agony of body and soul was more intense than his words could describe or we can imagine.

(g) Job's three friends identified the cause of Job's affliction as his sin. Elihu placed more emphasis on the sanctifying *purpose* of the affliction than on its *cause*. All four sought to justify God's ways. Job wished they had never broken their initial week-long silence. (Cf. 2:13; 13:5.)

(h) Job became more impatient and self-righteous as time passed. His afflictions intensified, and his friends were speaking more severely and critically. Although Job never cursed God to His face, as Satan had predicted (2:5), his words addressed to God were harsh and even bitter. His relationship to his Lord was at the lowest point when God began to speak to him out of the whirlwind.

2. Were you satisfied while studying chapters 3-37 that you were learning a true and dependable viewpoint on human suffering? If not, why not?

_____

_____

_____

Consider these comments:

Job and the others were trying to fit together the pieces of a puzzle without having all the pieces in their grasp. Consequently the book of Job is an eloquent commentary on the inadequacy of the human mind to reduce the complexity of the problem of suffering to some consistent pattern.[1]

3. If God is who the Bible says He is, can human despair in any situation be justified? Is there hope for a hardened sinner as long as there is breath? If so, on what does such a hope depend?

_____

_____

_____

Over what do Christians tend to despair?

_____

_____

Keep this in mind as you begin to study God's words to a despairing Job.

4. Recall from chapter 37 Elihu's many descriptions of an approaching storm ("whirlwind," 37:9).[2] How do those descriptions set the mood for the Lord's appearance (theophany) to Job "out of the whirlwind" (38:1)?

_____

_____

5. Read Job 9:1-9 and recall that Job recognized God as the sovereign creator and sustainer of the universe. He did not, however, relate his problem of suffering to this knowledge.

6. Record substitute readings in your Bible as shown in III. NOTES.

II. ANALYSIS

Segment to be analyzed: 38:1–40:5
Stanza divisions: at verses 38:1, 4, 8, 12, 16, 19, 22, 25, 31, 34, 39, 41; 39:1, 5, 9, 13, 19, 26; 40:1, 3

1. E. Heavenor, "Job," in *The New Bible Commentary*, p. 388.
2. The word "whirlwind" in 37:9 and 38:1 translates two different Hebrew words, but both are severe storms. Read Jeremiah 23:19 and Proverbs 1:27 for other appearances of the two words.

A. Opening Challenge: 38:1-3

1. What facts are established in verse 1? (You may be surprised at how many you find.)

_____

_____

_____

2. Is God referring to Elihu or to Job in the phrase, "Who is this?" (38:2)? Evaluate the arguments advanced to support the following views.

(a) Elihu is the person mentioned in 38:2. Morgan writes:

> While the whole speech was the answer of Jehovah to Job, the introductory question almost certainly referred to the speech of Elihu. The challenge [charged Elihu] with darkening counsel by the use of words which he himself did not perfectly understand.... His theme [God in nature] was too great for him, and God took it from him, and dealt with it Himself."[3]

(b) Job is the person in 38:2. This view is supported by (1) the fact that God makes no specific reference to Elihu in His speech; (2) the fact that verse 3, which is intimately related to verse 2, is clearly addressed to Job; (3) 34:35 and 35:16 refer to Job as speaking "without knowledge."

3. What tone of challenge do you sense in the words "Gird up now thy loins like a man" (38:3)?

_____

_____

It is interesting to observe that the Hebrew word for "man" used here is not one of the more common designations in the Old Testament. E. Heavenor writes, "The word *gebber* 'denotes man, not in frailty but in his strength, man as a combatant' (Strahan). Repeatedly Job had used language (e.g., xxxi. 35-37, xiii. 22) which seemed to suggest that in him God would find a worthy combatant. Ironically God takes him at his own valuation."[4]

But lest we see in the words of the Lord only a strong challenge, let us be reminded that the words "Gird up now thy loins" suggest divine exhortation as well. Morgan writes, "So far as circumstances were concerned, he [Job] is seen as a derelict, pos

---

3. G. Campbell Morgan, *The Book of Job*, p. 208.
4. E. Heavenor, "Job" in *The New Bible Commentary*, p. 408.

sessing nothing. The first words of God to him remind him that he still had his own personality."[5]

4. What does God demand of Job (38:3)?

_____

_____

B. The Speech: 38:4–39:30

1. First scan chapters 38 and 39 for general impressions. Observe the number of questions asked by God. God often answers man's questions by asking questions. Do you recall occasions when Jesus used this method (e.g., Mark 11:28-30; 12:14-16)?

_____

_____

2. As you study this discourse, look for:
    (a) *What* the Lord says.
    (b) *Why* He says it.
Let us first observe the *what*. The Lord speaks about inanimate creation (38:4-38) and then about animal creation (38:39–39:30). How does He bring Job into this discourse, as He refers to each of His creations? Use this as an example:

CREATION	JOB
I, God, laid the foundations. I made the measurements. I laid the cornerstone.	Where were you when I did these things? Who did these things if I didn't?

3. Note the four kinds of questions repeatedly asked of Job: Knowest thou?; Canst thou?; Hast thou?; Who hath? What answers does God expect to these rhetorical questions?

_____

What does this reveal about the *why* of God's discourse?

_____

_____

5. G. Campbell Morgan, *The Answers of Jesus to Job*, p. 102.

4. Do these words of God *specifically* answer Job's question about why the godly suffer?

C. God Repeats His Challenge: 40:1-2

Compare 40:2 with 38:2-3. According to 40:2, how had Job addressed God in his earlier speeches?

Had any of the three friends or Elihu accused Job of this?

Since this describes Job's heart at this time, what is his basic spiritual need?

What does this reveal about God's purpose in speaking as He does?

D. Job's Response: 40:3-5

1. Job immediately cries out, "Behold, I am nothing!" (The word "vile" as used in the KJV does not carry a moral connotation. The word means insignificant, of no account, of utter humiliation. Compare Deuteronomy 25:3 and Philippians 3:21 in Berkeley.) Is this what God wanted Job to see and admit?

If so, why?

Compare Psalm 8. Note the exclamation of the first and last verses, and the question of verse 4.

2. The four friends failed to reach Job, but God succeeded. Explain why.

_____

_____

3. If God did not specifically answer the problem on Job's mind, did He nevertheless answer Job? If so, how?

_____

_____

Would you say that Job's response lacks a spirit of repentance for sin? Keep in mind this question and your answer when you begin to study the next lesson.

III. NOTES

Mark these substitute readings (from the NASB) in your Bible before you begin your analysis.

	King James Version	Substitute Reading
38:10	brake up for it my decreed place	placed boundaries on it
12	dayspring	dawn
14	as clay to the seal	as clay under the seal
16	search of the depth	recesses of the deep
25	divided a watercourse	cleft a channel
32	Mazzaroth	a constellation
32	Arcturus with his sons	the Big and the Little Dipper (TEV)
39:1	hinds	deer
9	unicorn	wild ox
20	The glory of his nostrils	his majestic snorting
40:4	I am vile	I am insignificant

IV. FOR THOUGHT AND DISCUSSION

1. Explain how a true discovery of oneself leads to a discovery of who God is.

95

2. What value did Jesus place on the total life of a person? Read Mark 8:34-37; John 3:16.

3. Does a modern Christian who is enduring severe suffering have more revelation of God to undergird him than Job had? Consider the following remarks:

> Job had never heard that most impressive divine Word, which has given mankind the clearest vision of God . . . the Word of the cross. The vision of the God of nature made Job a worshipper. How much more ought the vision of the God of Calvary bring the sufferer to his knees, 'lost in wonder, love, and praise'![6]

4. "Without faith it is impossible to please [God]." Apply Hebrews 11:6 to the experience of suffering. Observe the references to physical suffering in Hebrews 11.

V. FURTHER STUDY

Recall as many instances as you can of God's appearing to His children, according to the biblical narrative. For example, how did God first reveal himself to Moses (Ex. 3:2)?

VI. WORDS TO PONDER

O Lord our God, the majesty and glory of your name fills all the earth and overflows the heavens. You have taught the little children to praise you perfectly (Ps. 8:1-2a, TLB).

6. E. Heavenor, "Job," in *The New Bible Commentary*, p. 409.

The Lord's Final Discourse

G od continues speaking to Job because Job has not yet repented of his sin of questioning God. "He must recognize not only the unreasonableness but also the sinfulness of criticizing the Almighty."[1] Job has admitted that he is of no account, utterly insignificant, in the vast and glorious realm of God's universe. But does he still think that there are flaws in God's ruling of the moral order? Job has acknowledged God's omnipotence and omniscience, but does he still question His justice? Definitely so, as our study of the biblical text will reveal.

I. PREPARATION FOR STUDY

1. Read descriptions of the behemoth and leviathan in a Bible dictionary.[2] The behemoth was probably a hippopotamus, whereas the leviathan was a gigantic species of crocodile.[3] Read the following verses that also refer to leviathan: Job 3:8*b* (NASB); 41:1; Psalm 74:14; 104:26; Isaiah 27:1.

2. Recall from your earlier studies that Job had ministered to his people as a judge before he was struck by tragedy (29:7-25). Do you think this "courtroom" experience may have contributed to his persistence in questioning God's justice?

---

1. Meredith G. Kline, "Job," in *the Wycliffe Bible Commentary*, p. 487.
2. The Hebrew word translated "behemoth" means literally "great beast." Its only appearance in the Bible is in Job 40:15.
3. Other identifications of behemoth and leviathan are elephant and whale, respectively.

II. ANALYSIS

Segment to be analyzed: 40:6–42:6
Stanza divisions: at verses 40:6, 10, 15, 19; 41:1, 12; 42:1

A. The Final Discourse of God: 40:6–41:34

This final discourse of God is a challenge (40:7) to Job by three approaches: by question (40:8-9), by invitation (40:10-14), and by illustration (40:15–34).

1. *By Question: 40:8-9*
What attribute of God had Job questioned, according to verse 8?

_____

What attribute does God extol in verse 9?

_____

What is the relationship between the attribute implied in verse 8 and those mentioned in verse 9?

_____

Can God have one attribute without the other? Justify your answer.

_____

_____

2. *By Invitation: 40:10-14*
God invites Job to prove that he knows how to exercise true justice. Is God suggesting that Job is able to perform this feat?

_____

Summarize the stanza in your own words.

_____

_____

_____

3. *By Illustration: 40:15–41:34*
God smites Job's presumptive spirit in yet another way. Study the lengthy descriptions of the two great monsters, to learn how God is saying, in effect: You can't control these animals (e.g., 41:1); how then can you stand before their Creator (41:10)? Applied more specifically to Job's problem, the two statements could be represented thus: You are ill equipped to hold sway over the material

world; you are even less equipped to hold sway over the moral order. Therefore, trust Me completely, even though you don't understand My ways.

B. Job's Repentance: 42:1-6

This short passage relates Job's peak spiritual experience in the book's drama. "In the hour of his bending he rose to kingship over the forces that had vexed and harassed him."[4] The ashes of mourning over physical trial (2:8) have been changed to ashes of repentance over spiritual corruption (42:6). Dim physical vision gives way to spiritual sight. Pride is slain, and God is glorified. What a beautiful picture.

1. Read verses 1-6 in *The Living Bible* and the *Amplified Bible*. Compare their readings with the suggestion that this paragraph is a conversation between Job and God, thus: Job, v. 2; God, v. 3*a*; Job, vv. 3*b*-4*a*; God, v. 4*b*; Job, vv. 5-6.
2. What bright contrast is made in 42:5?

Compare 23:3.

Now Job has truly found himself in relation to God. "Acquainted with God, his treasure was laid in the dust, and he had found Jehovah to be his all-sufficient strength."[5]
3. It is generally agreed that the greatest saints are those who know best their own sinfulness. Compare the contrition of Job with the experiences of Isaiah (Isa. 6:1-5) and Saul of Tarsus (Acts 9:3-9). Does Job repent for sins of which his friends had accused him? What does he confess?

---

4. G. Campbell Morgan, *The Book of Job*, p. 219.
5. Ibid.

III. FOR THOUGHT AND DISCUSSION

1. Job finally expresses the following convictions: "I know that thou canst do everything" (42:2); and "I abhor myself" (42:6). How do they answer his problem of suffering?

2. How would you describe true repentance?

3. Why is the teaching of Scripture a necessary ingredient in Christian counseling? Consider the following comments:

> The appearance of men to counsel Job leads to controversy, disillusionment and despair; the appearance of God leads to submission, faith and courage. The word of man is unable to penetrate the darkness of Job's mind; the Word of God brings abiding light. The God of the theophany does not answer any of the burning questions that are debated so hotly in the course of the book; but He answers the need of Job's heart. He does not explain each phase of the battle; but He makes Job more than conqueror in it.[6]

IV. WORDS TO PONDER

Then I knew only what others had told me, but now I have seen you with my own eyes (42:5, TEV).

---

6. E. Heavenor, "Job," in *The New Bible Commentary*, p. 388.

Lesson 13
Job's Restoration

The panoramic final scene in the drama of Job portrays the patriarch's glorious restoration. "So the Lord blessed the latter end of Job more than his beginning" (42:12*a*). Relating this verse to the full story of Job reveals a fundamental truth: God tests men in order to approve them. And when He approves them, He rewards them.

If 42:7-17 were not included, the book of Job would leave a host of unanswered questions. You may be surprised to learn how much of all that transpired in the other forty-one chapters is interpreted in this passage.

I. PREPARATION FOR STUDY

1. Review Chart E. and observe that this passage forms the epilogue of the book and shows the sequel to the prologue (1:1–2:13). Note that only the prologue and epilogue are written in prose.

2. Scan 1:1–2:13 in your Bible to review the events of that opening narrative.

3. Recall the crucial experiences of Job in chapters 1-41. These are listed in the left-hand column of Chart R.

The passage for this lesson is about Job's restoration (right-hand column). Scan the text now and note what the restoration involved. Record the experiences on Chart R. Observe among other things how the restoration paralleled the decline, in an inverse order.

II. ANALYSIS

Segment to be analyzed: 42:7-17
Paragraph divisions: at verses 7, 10

101

DECLINE chaps. 1-41	RESTORATION chap. 42
PERFECT AND UPRIGHT MAN 1:8	ACCEPTED BY THE LORD 42:9

(a) slandered by Satan before God   (f)

(b) wealth taken away   (e)

(c) children slain   (d)

(d) body plagued   (c)

(e) character minimized by friends   (b)

(f) JOB DOUBTS AND CHARGES GOD   (a) JOB CONFESSES AND REPENTS (42:1-6)

A. General Analysis

Read each paragraph and record a main theme for each.
42:7-9

_____

42:10-17

_____

B. Paragraph Analysis

1. *Paragraph 42:7-9*
What spiritual lessons do you learn here?

_____

_____

_____

_____

Recall that, when we were studying the speeches of Job's friends
(chaps. 4-37), we often referred to 42:7-9 for a true evaluation of
their counsel.

2. *Paragraph 42:10-17*

Compare Job's final blessing (42:10-17) to his earlier blessing (1:2-3).

_____

_____

_____

Is the believer who faithfully endures a spiritual trial always rewarded with material blessing? What underlying principle of reward is taught in this paragraph?

_____

_____

III. NOTES

1. *"Eliphaz . . . Bildad . . . Zophar"* (42:9). Only Job's three friends are mentioned in this passage. Consult commentaries for suggestions as to why Elihu is not included in this indictment.

2. *"The Lord also accepted Job"* (42:9). A literal translation is "The Lord lifted up the face of Job" (NASB, marg.).

3. *"Seven sons and three daughters"* (42:13). See 1:2. The names of the three daughters, recorded in verse 14, symbolize the beauty and glory of Job's restoration. The Hebrew names, in the order given, mean "dove," "cassia" (a perfume), and "beautifier" (lit., "horn of eye-paint"). Observe that Job's wife (cf. 2:9) is not mentioned in the epilogue.

4. *"Old and full of days"* (42:17). Compare Genesis 25:8; 35:29. If Job was around sixty years of age when he was afflicted, then he lived to be about two hundred (cf. 42:16).

IV. FOR THOUGHT AND DISCUSSION

1. Now that you have completed your study of Job, what are your thoughts about trials from the hand of God? Consider the following comments:

> Job was not meant to know the explanation of his trial. . . . If Job **had** known, there would have been no place for faith. . . . The Scriptures are as wise in their **reservations** as they are in their **revelations**. Enough is revealed to make faith intelligent. Enough is reserved to give faith scope for development.[1]

1. J. Sidlow Baxter, *Explore the Book*, vol. 3 (Grand Rapids: Zondervan, 1960), p. 27.

2. What Christian hymns dealing with trials can you recall?
Ponder the blessed truths of this stanza from "In the Hour of Trial," by James Montgomery:

> Should Thy mercy send me sorrow, toil, and woe;
> Or should pain attend me on my path below;
> Grant that I may never fail Thy hand to see;
> Grant that I may ever cast my care on Thee.

* * *

CONCLUSION

Two verses of James's epistle are part of God's inspired commentary on the book of Job:

Behold, we count those blessed who endured. You have
heard of the endurance of Job and have seen the outcome of the
Lord's dealings, that the Lord is full of compassion and is merciful
(5:11, NASB).

Blessed is a man who perseveres under trial; for once he has
been approved, he will receive the crown of life, which the Lord
has promised to those who love Him (1:12, NASB).

Bibliography

RESOURCES FOR FURTHER STUDY

Archer, Gleason L. *A Survey of Old Testament Introduction*. Chicago: Moody, 1964.
Blair, J. Allen. *Living Patiently*. Neptune, N.J.: Loizeaux, 1966. A devotional study.
Jensen, Irving L. *How to Profit from Bible Reading*. Chicago: Moody, 1985.
_____. *Independent Bible Study*. Chicago: Moody, 1963.
_____. *Jensen's Survey of the Old Testament*. Chicago: Moody, 1978.
Lewis, C. S. *The Problem of Pain*. New York: Macmillan, 1965.
Morgan, G. Campbell. *The Answers of Jesus to Job*. Westwood, N.J.: Revell, 1935.
New International Version Study Bible. Grand Rapids: Zondervan, 1985.
The Ryrie Study Bible. Chicago: Moody, 1985.
Tenney, Merrill C., ed. *The Zondervan Pictorial Bible Dictionary*. Grand Rapids: Zondervan, 1963.
Unger, Merrill F. *New Unger's Bible Handbook*. Chicago: Moody, 1984.

COMMENTARIES AND TOPICAL STUDIES

Delitzsch, F. *The Book of Job*. 2 vols. Grand Rapids: Eerdmans, 1949.
Heavenor, E. S. P. "Job." In *The New Bible Commentary*. Edited by F. Davidson. Grand Rapids: Eerdmans, 1953.
Kline, Meredith G. "Job." In *The Wycliffe Bible Commentary*. Edited by Charles F. Pfeiffer and Everett F. Harrison. Chicago: Moody, 1962.

Lange, John Peter. *Commentary on the Holy Scriptures,* "Job." Grand Rapids: Zondervan, n.d.

MacBeath, Andrew. *The Book of Job.* Grand Rapids: Baker, 1966.

Morgan, G. Campbell. *The Book of Job.* The Analyzed Bible. Westwood, N.J.: Revell, 1909.

Stedman, Ray C. *Expository Studies in Job: Behind Suffering.* Waco, Tex.: Word, 1981.

Zuck, Roy. *Job.* Everyman's Bible Commentary. Chicago: Moody, 1978.